BLOCKCHAIN BLUEPRINT

PROJECT MANAGEMENT STRATEGIES FOR FINTECH SUCCESS

Odunayo Akindote

ACEworld PGS

ISBN-13: 9789787701201

Cover design by: Mubby Creations

Published by: ACEworld PGS (aceworldpgs.com)

PREFACE

The financial landscape is undergoing a seismic shift, one driven by groundbreaking innovations that promise to redefine how we transact, manage assets, and interact within the global financial ecosystem. In the midst of this transformation lie two pivotal forces: blockchain technology and financial technology, or fintech. These technologies are no longer fringe ideas but are becoming foundational pillars in the modern economy. "Blockchain Blueprint: Project Management Strategies for Fintech Success" was conceived as a comprehensive guide to help both industry veterans and newcomers navigate the unique challenges and immense opportunities at the intersection of blockchain and fintech.

In the pages that follow, you'll journey through a digital world where decentralized systems and tamper-proof ledgers challenge traditional models of finance. You'll gain insights into the fundamental concepts of blockchain, understand its impact on financial services, and explore the role it plays in enhancing security, transparency, and efficiency within fintech. As we delve deeper, you will discover the ways blockchain empowers financial solutions, from cross-border payments and smart contracts to decentralized finance (DeFi) platforms that aim to democratize access to financial services globally.

However, despite the promise blockchain holds, successful implementation in the fintech sector requires more than just a great idea. The complexities inherent in blockchain projects such as technical, regulatory, and organizational, demand skilled project management to guide them to fruition. This book offers a blueprint for managing these projects, covering key areas such as defining project scope, resource allocation, risk mitigation, and regulatory compliance, all specifically tailored to blockchain's nuances. Effective project management in this domain isn't just a tool for success; it's the cornerstone that allows us to realize the true potential of blockchain within fintech.

As you read, remember that your work in this field contributes to shaping the future of finance. The insights and strategies you'll encounter here are designed not only to help you manage projects successfully but also to inspire a bold vision for the role blockchain can play in the financial world. Embrace this journey with courage and creativity, knowing that you stand on the frontier of a revolution that is only just beginning.

ACKNOWLEDGEMENT

First and foremost, I want to give all glory and honor to God. Your grace and guidance have been my constant source of strength, clarity, and purpose. Through every challenge and triumph, You have been my foundation, and without Your unwavering love and wisdom, this work would not have been possible.

To my incredible mother, Mercy Akindote, no words can truly capture the depth of my gratitude. You have been my rock, my cheerleader, and my confidante. Your sacrifices, wisdom, and endless support have shaped me into the person I am today. Your encouragement gave me the confidence to pursue my dreams, and your resilience taught me the value of perseverance. I am so blessed to have a mother as strong and caring as you, and I dedicate this achievement to you.

To my family and friends, your love and belief in me kept me motivated throughout this journey. Thank you for being there in moments of doubt, for celebrating the small victories, and for offering words of wisdom when I needed them most.

Finally, to everyone who contributed to the completion of this project, whether through support, inspiration, or shared experiences, thank you. This work stands on the shoulders of so many, and I am grateful for each of you.

INTRODUCTION

The financial world is undergoing a profound transformation, driven by the emergence of innovative technologies that promise to redefine how we conduct transactions, manage assets, and interact with financial institutions. At the heart of this transformation are two powerful forces: blockchain technology and financial technology, or fintech. This book, "Blockchain Blueprint: Project Management Strategies for Fintech Success," aims to equip you with the knowledge and strategies needed to harness these technologies effectively, whether you're a seasoned professional or just starting your journey.

What is Blockchain?

To understand blockchain, imagine a digital ledger that records transactions in a way that is secure, transparent, and tamper-proof. Unlike traditional ledgers maintained by a central authority, blockchain operates on a decentralized network of computers, known as nodes. Each node maintains a copy of the entire ledger, ensuring that no single entity has control over the data. This decentralization is a key feature that enhances security and trust among users.

A blockchain is composed of a series of blocks, each containing a list of transactions. These blocks are linked together using cryptographic hashes, forming an unalterable chain. Once a block is added to the chain, the information it contains is permanent and cannot be changed without altering all subsequent blocks—a task that would require the consensus of the majority of the network.

The concept of blockchain was first introduced with Bitcoin in 2008, a digital currency that operates without the need for a central bank. Bitcoin showcased blockchain's potential to enable peer-to-peer transactions, reducing the need for intermediaries and lowering transaction costs. Since then, the technology has evolved, finding applications across various sectors, including supply chain management, healthcare, and, most notably, fintech.

The Rise of Fintech and its Intersection with Blockchain

Fintech is remoulding the financial services industry by leveraging technology to improve and automate processes. From mobile banking and digital wallets to crowdfunding and investment platforms, fintech solutions are making financial services more accessible, efficient, and user-friendly. The rise of fintech is driven by a desire to meet the changing expectations of consumers who demand faster, more convenient, and more transparent services.

Blockchain technology complements fintech by providing the underlying infrastructure needed to enhance security, transparency, and efficiency. For instance, blockchain can streamline cross-border payments, reducing the time and cost associated with traditional banking systems. It can also enable smart contracts—self-executing contracts with the terms of the agreement directly written into code—thereby automating complex financial transactions without the need for intermediaries.

Moreover, blockchain's ability to create a decentralized and immutable record of transactions is paving the way for new fintech innovations, such as decentralized finance (DeFi) platforms, which offer financial services without relying on traditional banks. These platforms are democratizing access to financial services, allowing anyone with an internet connection to participate in the global financial system.

The Importance of Project Management in Blockchain Implementations

While the potential of blockchain in fintech is immense, successfully implementing blockchain projects requires careful planning and execution. This is where project management becomes crucial. Effective project management ensures that blockchain initiatives are delivered on time, within budget, and meet the desired quality standards.

Blockchain projects often involve complex technical challenges, regulatory considerations, and the need for cross-functional collaboration. Project managers play a vital role in navigating these complexities, coordinating efforts across teams, managing risks, and ensuring that all stakeholders are aligned toward common objectives.

In this book, we will explore project management strategies specifically tailored for blockchain projects in the fintech sector. We will cover essential topics such as defining project scope and objectives, managing resources, mitigating risks, and ensuring compliance with regulatory requirements. By providing a comprehensive blueprint for project management, this book aims to empower you to lead successful blockchain initiatives and drive innovation in the fintech industry.

As you flip the pages of this book, remember that the world of blockchain and fintech is rapidly evolving. By mastering the art of project management, you can position yourself at the forefront of this exciting transformation, creating value and driving change in the digital economy.

CONTENTS

CHAPTER 1: Blockchain Fundamentals for Project Managers

Blockchain is often seen as a mysterious and highly technical concept, especially for project managers who are more familiar with traditional IT or finance project management techniques. However, as fintech evolves, understanding blockchain is essential for ensuring the success of future financial technologies. Practically, blockchain is a decentralized, digital ledger technology designed to record and store data in a way that is immutable (unchangeable) and transparent. It has the power to change not just finance but industries such as healthcare, supply chain, and real estate. However, for fintech, blockchain brings particular relevance due to its ability to provide secure, efficient, and transparent transaction mechanisms.

As a project manager, it's essential to understand blockchain's core principles, how it works, and why it's rapidly gaining attention across industries. This knowledge will not only help you lead blockchain-based projects but also enable you to effectively communicate with technical teams and stakeholders who may be less familiar with the technology.

Key Components of Blockchain Technology

1. Distributed Ledger Technology (DLT):

At the heart of blockchain is the concept of a distributed ledger. Unlike traditional databases that are maintained by a central authority (like a bank or government), blockchain is maintained by a network of computers (or nodes) that each have a copy of the entire ledger. This distributed nature ensures that no single entity controls the data, making the system more resilient to fraud, hacking, or data loss. The ledger is constantly updated, meaning that any changes (or transactions) made are instantly visible across the entire network.

Why it matters for Project Managers:

As a project manager, the decentralized nature of blockchain technology requires a fundamental shift in how projects are structured and managed. In traditional IT systems, project managers deal with centralized systems where clear hierarchies exist, and decisions can be made by a single authority. Blockchain changes this dynamic. You'll now be dealing with multiple stakeholders, perhaps even across borders, where authority is distributed across nodes in a network.

This means decision-making processes could become more democratic or consensus-based, which might slow down certain aspects of the project but improve transparency and trust among participants. You'll need to ensure that each stakeholder understands their role within this decentralized framework, and the project's success will depend on how well you coordinate communication and cooperation across this distributed network.

Moreover, the security and reliability of a distributed ledger reduce concerns about data integrity and single points of failure. However, it also introduces new challenges related to ensuring all nodes in the network stay synchronized. Monitoring the consistency and reliability of data across multiple nodes adds an extra layer of complexity, requiring you to develop more advanced tracking, testing, and risk management protocols.

Finally, the transparency of blockchain networks means that all participants can see changes in real time. While this promotes accountability, it can also expose vulnerabilities quickly. As a project manager, you'll need to be prepared to manage these transparency expectations, balancing the need for open access with the potential risks of exposing sensitive or competitive data.

2. Consensus Algorithms:

For a blockchain to function effectively, there must be a way for the network of nodes to agree on which transactions are valid. This is where consensus algorithms come in. The two most common consensus mechanisms are Proof of Work (PoW) and Proof of Stake (PoS):

- **Proof of Work (PoW):** This algorithm requires nodes to solve complex mathematical puzzles in order to validate transactions and add them to the blockchain. It's used by popular blockchains like Bitcoin and Ethereum (though Ethereum has recently transitioned to PoS).

- **Proof of Stake (PoS):** This algorithm, in contrast, allows nodes to validate transactions based on how many coins or tokens they "stake" or lock in the system, reducing the need for intensive computational power.

Why it matters for Project Managers:

The choice of consensus algorithm directly impacts the overall project in terms of cost, resources, timeline, and risk management. PoW, for example, is known for being highly secure, but it comes at the expense of massive computational power and energy consumption. If your project utilizes a PoW-based blockchain, you'll need to account for these significant resource demands, which could inflate costs and slow down project timelines. Your resource allocation plan will need to include strategies to manage these demands—whether it's securing energy-efficient hardware or sourcing renewable energy solutions to minimize environmental impact.

On the other hand, PoS blockchains are less resource-intensive and faster, which can allow for more streamlined operations. However, the project risks and security considerations differ. PoS relies on the amount of staked cryptocurrency, which introduces potential vulnerabilities like centralization risks, where wealthier participants hold disproportionate control. As a project manager, you'll need to weigh these risks against the needs of your project. Additionally, you'll need to ensure that the technical team has a solid understanding of the chosen consensus model, as any vulnerabilities in the staking process could undermine the blockchain's integrity.

Understanding the nuances of these algorithms also allows you to manage expectations with stakeholders better. Clients and non-technical team members may not be familiar with the complexities of consensus mechanisms, and part of your role will be to explain how these systems impact performance, costs, and security. Anticipating these questions will allow you to provide clear, confident explanations, making sure that every stakeholder understands why a particular consensus mechanism was chosen and how it aligns with the project's overall goals.

3. Smart Contracts:

One of the most groundbreaking innovations of blockchain technology is the concept of smart contracts. A smart contract is a self-executing contract where the terms of the agreement are directly written into lines of code. Once certain predefined conditions are met, the contract automatically executes. This eliminates the need for intermediaries (like lawyers or notaries) and can drastically speed up processes like loans, insurance claims, or property sales.

Why it matters for Project Managers:

Smart contracts offer the potential to automate significant parts of your project's workflow, reducing the need for manual intervention and cutting down on human error. For example, in a fintech project, you could automate the release of funds, delivery of assets, or execution of transactions without relying on a third-party intermediary. This can improve project efficiency and reduce costs, but it also introduces a new set of responsibilities for project managers.

Since smart contracts are essentially "code-as-law," the accuracy of that code is paramount. Any bugs, errors, or incomplete conditions could result in catastrophic financial losses or legal disputes. As the project manager, you'll need to ensure that the team working on smart contract development is not only technically proficient but also understands the business logic and legal implications embedded within these contracts. Rigorous testing will be required before deployment to avoid the risk of faulty execution.

Additionally, while smart contracts offer a high level of

automation, they may require integration with legacy systems, third-party platforms, or even other blockchain networks. Managing these integrations will be crucial to the project's success. You'll need to ensure compatibility, security, and reliability when smart contracts interact with external entities or systems. Stakeholder education is also critical here—many stakeholders may be unfamiliar with the idea of "self-executing" contracts, so part of your role will involve demystifying the technology and clarifying how it aligns with business objectives.

4. Public vs. Private Blockchains:

There are two major types of blockchains: public and private. Public blockchains, like Bitcoin and Ethereum, are open for anyone to join and participate in. They are fully decentralized, meaning that no single entity controls them. Private blockchains, on the other hand, are restricted and controlled by specific organizations or consortia. They are commonly used in industries like banking, where privacy and security are paramount.

Why it matters for Project Managers:

The decision between using a public or private blockchain will have significant implications for the project's architecture, governance, and scalability. Public blockchains are typically more decentralized and transparent, offering a high degree of trust and auditability, which might be a selling point for certain fintech applications. However, because they are open to the public, they can also be harder to control, slower due to network congestion, and subject to regulatory scrutiny. Managing a project on a public blockchain may require you to consider factors like governance models, user incentives, and network security on a much larger scale.

In contrast, private blockchains offer more control to the organization, allowing you to restrict access, define custom rules, and optimize performance for specific use cases. However, these benefits come with trade-offs in decentralization and scalability. You may need to manage the complexities of creating a permissioned environment that balances security with accessibility, especially if multiple organizations or consortiums are involved. As a project manager, your role will involve negotiating these trade-offs and ensuring that the choice of blockchain aligns with the broader business goals, particularly in sectors like finance where compliance and data privacy are critical.

Additionally, managing a private blockchain means you'll often need to deal with governance structures—how decisions are made, who has control, and how disputes are resolved. Developing a strong governance framework will be key to avoiding issues down the line. You'll also need to ensure that all stakeholders understand the limitations of private blockchains in terms of scalability and future integration with public networks if the project evolves in that direction.

Blockchain's Impact on Fintech

Blockchain, without a doubt, is rapidly transforming the financial technology (fintech) sector in several profound ways, offering greater efficiency, transparency, security, and decentralization. As fintech companies explore new ways to innovate traditional financial services, blockchain is becoming the key enabler for many of these transformative solutions. Below are the major areas where blockchain is reshaping the fintech industry, and why understanding its impact is crucial for project managers.

1. Cross-Border Payments

Traditionally, cross-border payments are time-consuming, expensive, and riddled with intermediaries. A single international transfer could take days to process due to the involvement of multiple banks, clearinghouses, and payment systems. Additionally, transaction fees are often high, making the process inefficient and costly for businesses and consumers alike.

Blockchain's Impact:

Blockchain technology enables peer-to-peer (P2P) transfers across borders without the need for intermediaries. Transactions can be processed in real-time or near real-time, drastically reducing processing times from days to seconds. For example, Ripple's blockchain-based solution, RippleNet, allows financial institutions to settle cross-border payments with end-to-end tracking and at significantly lower fees. This makes cross-border transactions faster, cheaper, and more transparent.

Blockchain's decentralized nature means that financial institutions can cut out the middlemen (like correspondent banks) and operate with fewer delays. Additionally, transaction details are securely encrypted, providing a more secure method of transferring funds across borders. This shift is particularly significant for fintech companies dealing with international clients or financial services.

Why it matters for Project Managers:

If your project involves international money transfers, blockchain can reduce costs and speed up delivery times. As a project manager, understanding the regulatory landscape in different countries becomes crucial. While blockchain simplifies cross-border payments, it still has to comply with varying financial regulations globally. Navigating these regulations and working with legal teams will be critical to ensuring your project's success. You'll also need to manage expectations about how blockchain-based payments will impact the user experience, as the benefits of speed and cost savings need to be balanced with potential integration challenges.

2. Decentralized Finance (DeFi)

Decentralized Finance, or DeFi, is one of the most disruptive innovations powered by blockchain. DeFi eliminates the need for traditional financial intermediaries (like banks or brokerages) by offering financial services such as lending, borrowing, trading, and earning interest on digital assets directly through blockchain technology. These services are driven by decentralized applications (dApps) and smart contracts, allowing users to interact with financial protocols without relying on centralized entities.

Blockchain's Impact:

DeFi allows users to participate in financial markets globally without the need for intermediaries, often providing higher returns and lower fees than traditional financial institutions. Platforms like Aave, Compound, and Uniswap enable users to borrow, lend, and trade digital assets, all governed by smart contracts that automate these financial processes. These protocols create an open, permissionless financial system where anyone with internet access can participate.

Additionally, DeFi unlocks new financial products like algorithmic stablecoins, decentralized exchanges, and yield farming, which provide innovative ways for users to maximize their capital in the blockchain ecosystem. However, the decentralized nature of DeFi also presents risks, such as smart contract vulnerabilities, a lack of consumer protection, and susceptibility to hacks and market manipulation.

Why it matters for Project Managers:

Managing a DeFi project can be incredibly complex. Project managers need to prioritize security since smart contract vulnerabilities can lead to significant financial losses. As the project manager, you will need to ensure that rigorous testing and auditing protocols are in place to prevent flaws in the code from being exploited. Additionally, (at the time of writing this book), DeFi operates in a largely unregulated space, which means legal and compliance risks are higher. Understanding the regulatory framework—or lack thereof—in the jurisdictions where your project operates will be essential.

From a project scope perspective, DeFi projects can grow rapidly due to their open nature, requiring agile and scalable management strategies. You'll also need to be ready for volatility, as decentralized financial systems are still in their infancy and can experience rapid changes in user behavior or external market conditions.

3. Tokenization of Assets

Tokenization refers to the process of converting real-world

assets—such as real estate, commodities, or even art—into digital tokens that exist on a blockchain. These tokens can represent ownership, rights, or other attributes and can be traded or exchanged on blockchain platforms.

Blockchain's Impact:

Blockchain makes it possible to break down illiquid assets into smaller, tradable tokens. This means that instead of buying an entire property or a piece of art, investors can purchase fractional ownership through tokens. For example, a $1 million property could be tokenized into 1 million tokens, allowing investors to buy, sell, or trade fractional ownership on blockchain-based marketplaces.

Tokenization opens new markets for investors who previously didn't have access to high-value assets due to capital constraints or geographical limitations. It also increases liquidity in traditionally illiquid markets like real estate, offering a more seamless way for investors to diversify their portfolios.

Why it matters for Project Managers:

Projects involving tokenized assets require a solid understanding of both blockchain and the underlying asset markets. As a project manager, you'll need to coordinate with legal, financial, and technical teams to ensure that tokens accurately represent the real-world assets they are tied to. This includes ensuring compliance with securities regulations, which vary by jurisdiction and can impact how tokens are issued, traded, and managed.

Additionally, you'll need to manage the integration of

tokenization platforms with existing financial systems or marketplaces, ensuring smooth workflows for buying, selling, and transferring tokens. Keeping stakeholders informed about the complexities of token standards (like ERC-20 or ERC-721) and how they impact project development will also be a key part of your role.

4. Fraud Prevention and Security

Financial fraud and security breaches are major concerns for any fintech company. Traditional financial systems are vulnerable to hacking, phishing, and other types of fraud due to centralized data storage and control.

Blockchain's Impact:

Blockchain's decentralized and cryptographic nature makes it an effective tool for preventing fraud. Since the blockchain ledger is immutable, it is nearly impossible for hackers to alter or delete transaction data once it has been validated and recorded. Furthermore, transactions are verified by consensus among multiple nodes, making it highly secure against single points of failure or attacks.

Blockchain can also enhance identity verification processes, making it easier to authenticate users and prevent fraud in transactions, lending, or investment activities. By using decentralized identity systems, blockchain can eliminate the need for third-party authentication services, thereby reducing the risk of identity theft.

Why it matters for Project Managers:

Blockchain-based fintech projects often prioritize security and fraud prevention as key selling points. As a project manager, you'll need to ensure that security is built into every stage of the project, from development to deployment. This involves coordinating regular security audits, working with cryptography experts, and staying informed about emerging threats in the blockchain ecosystem.

Additionally, blockchain's promise of fraud prevention may require you to communicate effectively with stakeholders about its advantages and limitations. While blockchain significantly reduces the likelihood of tampering, it is not immune to all forms of fraud, such as phishing attacks or vulnerabilities in smart contracts. Managing these expectations and ensuring that security measures evolve with the project will be crucial.

Blockchain is much more than a buzzword in the fintech world. Its ability to decentralize control, provide transparency, and enhance security offers immense value to project managers navigating fintech's fast-paced landscape. The combination of distributed ledgers, consensus algorithms, and smart contracts brings transformative changes to how financial services are built, operated, and optimized.

For project managers, understanding these key components is the first step in effectively leading blockchain-based initiatives. As we've explored, the decentralization of data and consensus-driven validation processes requires a shift from traditional project management approaches. Whether dealing with public or private blockchains, the implications on project scope, resources, and timelines are significant.

Blockchain's impact on fintech is already evident in areas like cross-border payments, decentralized finance, and asset tokenization. These applications are unlocking new efficiencies and opportunities, but they also introduce new challenges—particularly in the areas of security and regulation. As you guide your teams through this evolving technological space, staying informed about these developments will be crucial.

With these foundational concepts in mind, you're ready to explore more in-depth strategies for managing blockchain projects within fintech. The journey continues with practical approaches for successfully navigating the complexities of this dynamic and transformative technology.

CHAPTER 2: Core Project Management Strategies

For fintech, where technology and finance connect, managing a project efficiently is key to its success. A well-structured project management strategy provides a roadmap that ensures clarity, coordination, and timely delivery. But what exactly are "core project management strategies," and how do they apply to blockchain and fintech?

Core project management strategies involve the basic principles and approaches that govern how a project is initiated, planned, executed, monitored, and completed. These strategies include defining project goals, identifying stakeholders, setting timelines, and managing resources—all while ensuring that the project aligns with broader business objectives.

In the context of blockchain, these strategies are even more crucial because blockchain projects often involve emerging technologies, regulatory challenges, and complex integrations. The decentralized and immutable nature of blockchain also requires a rethinking of how we approach both planning and execution. Let's examine the core strategies that every fintech professional must master to manage blockchain projects effectively.

1. Clear Goal Definition and Scope Management

The first step in any project management strategy is setting clear goals. For a blockchain-based fintech project, this means identifying what the technology will accomplish. Is it a decentralized application (DApp)? A smart contract platform? A new digital asset solution? Having a precise goal helps prevent scope creep—the tendency for project objectives to shift and expand over time, leading to delays and cost overruns.

Example: Imagine a blockchain project aimed at improving cross-border payment systems. The primary goal might be to reduce transaction times from days to minutes. Keeping this goal in focus ensures that any additional features (such as integrating additional cryptocurrencies) are evaluated carefully to avoid straying from the main objective.

Scope management is equally critical. In blockchain projects, the scope can easily expand as the team discovers new use cases or technical challenges arise. To combat this, project managers need a robust process for evaluating changes and determining their impact on timelines, resources, and deliverables.

2. Stakeholder Engagement and Communication

Stakeholder management is the backbone of any successful project, and it's even more important in blockchain projects due to its highly collaborative and often decentralized nature. Key stakeholders may include:

- Developers and technical teams
- Regulatory bodies
- Investors and business leaders
- End-users (customers)

Effective communication ensures that all parties are aligned, from technical feasibility to regulatory compliance. Engaging stakeholders early and frequently helps to build trust and provides opportunities for input, which is crucial in the iterative nature of blockchain projects.

Regular Updates: Because fintech and blockchain industries evolve rapidly, project managers should establish a communication cadence (e.g., weekly or bi-weekly updates) that keeps all parties informed about progress, risks, and potential changes.

Decision-Making: Blockchain projects often require cross-functional decisions—should the project adopt a public blockchain (like Ethereum) or a private, permissioned one? These choices should involve input from stakeholders who understand the technology and the broader business goals.

3. Risk Management and Compliance in Blockchain Projects

Every project carries risk, but blockchain projects have unique risks due to their technical, legal, and regulatory complexities. Managing these risks is essential to ensuring that blockchain projects are delivered on time and within budget.

Technical Risks: Blockchain involves cutting-edge technologies that are still evolving. Security vulnerabilities (e.g., 51% attacks, smart contract bugs) and scalability issues (like network congestion) are critical risks.

Mitigation Strategy: Regular code audits, security testing, and working with blockchain experts to ensure best practices.

Regulatory Risks: Blockchain operates in a fluid regulatory landscape. Governments around the world are still deciding how to regulate cryptocurrencies and blockchain-based services, so projects might face compliance issues that change mid-project.

Mitigation Strategy: Monitor regulatory updates closely and consult legal experts in fintech to ensure that your project adheres to local and international regulations.

Market Risks: The volatility of the cryptocurrency market can impact the value of tokens or digital assets being developed. This affects investor confidence and project funding.

Mitigation Strategy: Diversifying project funding sources and creating a financial plan that anticipates market fluctuations.

4. Resource and Time Management

In blockchain, time is money—literally. With the rise of decentralized finance (DeFi), projects must move quickly to capture market opportunities. Effective resource and time management are key to maintaining momentum without sacrificing quality.

Agile Resource Allocation: Blockchain development often involves a blend of full-time employees, contractors, and external vendors. To maximize efficiency, it's important to allocate resources flexibly, based on the current project phase. During initial prototyping, you may need more developers; during the testing phase, you may require more auditors and testers.

Time Management Tools: Leveraging tools like Gantt charts, Agile sprints, or Kanban boards can help fintech project managers track milestones and ensure timely delivery. In blockchain projects, breaking down tasks into small, manageable segments (like developing a smart contract or integrating a specific API) makes it easier to manage the project's complexity.

5. Adapting to Technological and Market Changes

Blockchain is a fast-paced industry with new platforms, protocols, and innovations emerging almost daily. A core project management strategy is building flexibility into the project plan to adapt to these changes without disrupting the overall vision.

Continuous Learning and Research: Project managers need to stay up-to-date on blockchain trends and technologies. Whether it's Ethereum upgrading to a new consensus mechanism or the rise of new Layer-2 scaling solutions, awareness of these developments allows you to adapt your project as necessary.

Pilot Programs and Testing: Before fully launching a blockchain application, many fintech companies roll out pilot programs. These smaller-scale versions of the final product allow the team to test assumptions, gather feedback, and identify technical issues early.

Traditional vs. Agile Project Management in Fintech

Now that we've covered core project management strategies,

it's important to understand how different methodologies fit into the fintech landscape. Two major project management methodologies dominate: **Traditional (Waterfall)** and **Agile**. Each has its strengths and is suited to different types of projects, including blockchain implementations in fintech. Let's break down these methodologies and explore which might be best suited for your blockchain-based project.

Traditional (Waterfall) Project Management

The Waterfall approach is the classic, linear project management methodology that follows a structured, sequential flow. In Waterfall, each phase of the project —planning, design, development, testing, and deployment— must be completed before moving on to the next. This method relies heavily on upfront planning and documentation, aiming to minimize changes once the project is in motion. It's considered ideal for projects where the scope and requirements are well-defined from the outset.

Key Characteristics of Waterfall:

1. Sequential Phases: In the Waterfall method, every phase depends on the completion of the previous one. For instance, a project moves from design to development only when the design phase is entirely complete, minimizing the possibility of revisiting earlier stages without significant cost. This structure provides a clear project roadmap but limits flexibility once a phase is locked in.

2. Extensive Documentation: Documentation is a cornerstone of Waterfall project management. Every step is thoroughly documented, from initial requirements to final deployment. This comprehensive approach ensures stakeholders remain aligned and serves as a reference for the project's progress.

3. Fixed Scope and Timeline: Waterfall projects typically begin with a fixed scope, budget, and timeline. Once the project requirements are set, there is little room for scope changes without disrupting the entire workflow. This makes it highly predictable but rigid, which can be challenging for projects where new requirements might emerge mid-development.

Pros of Waterfall:

Clear Structure and Predictability: Waterfall's rigid structure provides clarity on timelines, budgets, and deliverables. Because each phase is completed before moving on to the next, project managers can easily track progress and manage risks. For highly regulated industries like fintech, this predictability can be critical.

Regulatory Compliance: In industries like fintech, where compliance with regulatory frameworks is mandatory, Waterfall's extensive documentation and structured nature are beneficial. The step-by-step process ensures that all regulatory checkpoints are met before advancing, reducing the risk of non-compliance.

Well-Suited for Established Technologies: For projects involving established, well-understood systems (such as internal blockchain auditing tools or compliance systems), Waterfall may be an ideal fit. Since the technology and processes are stable, it's easier to map out the project from start to finish without needing mid-project adjustments.

Cons of Waterfall:

Inflexibility in Changing Environments: In a rapidly evolving space like fintech, where blockchain technologies and regulations shift frequently, Waterfall's fixed scope and limited flexibility can become a hindrance. Once the project has begun, it's costly and time-consuming to pivot or incorporate new features.

Difficulty Accommodating Innovation: Blockchain technology, particularly in decentralized finance (DeFi), is still evolving. Waterfall's rigid, phased approach may slow down innovative projects that require iterative development or the ability to adapt to new market demands quickly.

Use Case for Waterfall in Blockchain Fintech Projects:

Waterfall can still play a valuable role in certain blockchain-based fintech projects. For example, if you're building an internal, blockchain-based transaction audit system for a traditional bank, where security and compliance are critical, the clear structure of Waterfall could be highly beneficial. In this scenario, the scope is well understood, and the need for rigorous documentation outweighs the need for flexibility. The regulatory environment may also favor a structured, step-by-step process, ensuring each phase meets legal and compliance standards.

However, for projects that deal with open blockchain ecosystems or rapidly evolving fintech products, Waterfall may prove too rigid to accommodate the fast pace of change.

Agile Project Management

Agile project management is designed to handle complex,

fast-moving projects by using an iterative approach. Rather than following a linear sequence, Agile breaks the project into smaller, manageable sprints, typically lasting two to four weeks. At the end of each sprint, teams deliver a functional piece of the project, allowing for continuous feedback and adjustments. This methodology is particularly well-suited for blockchain projects in fintech, where rapid development, iteration, and feedback are critical.

Key Characteristics of Agile:

1. Iterative Development: Agile emphasizes continuous iteration, where development happens in incremental sprints. Each sprint delivers a working product or feature, which can then be tested, reviewed, and refined based on feedback from stakeholders or end-users.

2. Continuous Feedback and Adaptation: One of Agile's strongest advantages is the ability to incorporate feedback at the end of every sprint. This allows the project to adapt quickly to changing requirements, user needs, or regulatory developments—an essential trait in the fast-paced fintech sector.

3. Flexibility in Scope: Unlike Waterfall, Agile thrives on adaptability. Teams can pivot or adjust their objectives as new challenges arise. This is particularly valuable in blockchain-based fintech projects, where market conditions, user demands, and regulatory environments can shift unexpectedly.

Pros of Agile:

Adaptability to Change: Agile's flexible nature is particularly beneficial in blockchain projects where change is inevitable.

The rapid pace of innovation in blockchain means that projects must evolve continuously, making Agile's iterative process a natural fit.

Increased Collaboration: Agile encourages frequent communication between developers, stakeholders, and end-users. This ongoing dialogue ensures that the project stays aligned with business goals and customer needs, reducing the risk of costly misalignment.

Quick Time-to-Market: Agile allows teams to deliver a minimum viable product (MVP) early in the development process, enabling quicker time-to-market. For blockchain fintech startups, this is crucial in staying competitive and capturing market share in a fast-moving industry.

Cons of Agile:

Requires Strong Collaboration and Commitment: Agile relies heavily on frequent collaboration and stakeholder involvement. For larger organizations or projects with multiple external stakeholders (such as regulatory bodies), this level of constant communication can be difficult to maintain.

Less Predictable Timelines: While Agile excels at delivering rapid iterations, it often lacks the timeline predictability of Waterfall. Because requirements evolve throughout the project, it can be challenging to predict when the project will be fully complete or how much it will ultimately cost.

Use Case for Agile in Blockchain Fintech Projects: Agile is ideal for blockchain projects that operate in fast-paced environments where innovation is crucial. For example, if you're developing a decentralized finance (DeFi) platform or a cryptocurrency wallet, Agile enables you to release features incrementally, gather user feedback, and rapidly adapt to market trends or new regulatory requirements. Blockchain projects that deal with public networks, decentralized apps (dApps), or rapidly changing fintech landscapes benefit significantly from Agile's flexibility and speed.

Agile's adaptability also makes it an excellent choice when dealing with blockchain regulations that are still being defined, allowing projects to incorporate legal and compliance changes without major disruption.

Which Approach is Better for Blockchain Projects?

While both Waterfall and Agile have their merits, Agile tends to be better suited for blockchain-based fintech projects. Blockchain projects often operate in environments where innovation, market conditions, and user requirements evolve rapidly—conditions that Agile is designed to handle. Agile's iterative nature allows blockchain teams to deliver functional products early, incorporate feedback, and adapt to new challenges, making it a better fit for decentralized applications, smart contract development, and DeFi platforms.

However, Waterfall can still be effective in certain blockchain fintech projects, particularly where compliance, security, and well-established processes are the top priorities. Some organizations even adopt **hybrid approaches** like **Agile-Waterfall**, combining Waterfall's structured planning with Agile's flexibility. This hybrid model can start with a solid, well-documented project foundation but evolve as the project progresses, allowing for adjustments as needed.

In summary, the choice between Waterfall and Agile depends on the specific nature of the blockchain project, the organization's regulatory needs, and the level of innovation required.

Key Considerations When Managing Blockchain-Based Projects

Managing blockchain projects presents a range of challenges that often surpass traditional project management practices. Due to its decentralized and immutable nature, blockchain technology demands a deep understanding of its intricacies, including technical constraints, regulatory implications, and its potential benefits within fintech. Below are the essential considerations for project managers overseeing blockchain-based initiatives:

1. Understanding the Technology

Blockchain is not a singular, uniform technology; it comes in multiple forms, each with distinct attributes. A solid grasp of these variations is crucial to aligning the technology with the project's goals.

Public Blockchains: Public blockchains like Bitcoin and Ethereum are decentralized and open to anyone, making them ideal for projects that prioritize transparency and open participation. Use cases include cryptocurrency platforms and decentralized finance (DeFi) applications, where trustlessness and verifiability are key.

Private Blockchains: In contrast, private blockchains, such as Hyperledger Fabric, are permissioned networks where only authorized participants can engage. These are commonly used in industries like banking, healthcare, and supply chain management, where control, privacy, and speed are critical concerns.

Choosing the Right Blockchain Type:

The decision between public and private blockchain infrastructure is pivotal. Public blockchains offer a higher degree of transparency and decentralization but come with trade-offs in terms of slower transaction speeds, higher operational costs, and scalability issues. Private blockchains, while more efficient and faster, may compromise on decentralization but are often better suited for projects requiring controlled access and confidentiality.

Key questions to ask when selecting a blockchain type:

- How important is transparency and decentralization for your project?

- Are privacy, speed, and control bigger priorities than public participation?

- What are the anticipated transaction volumes, and what is the cost sensitivity?

2. Regulatory and Compliance Factors

The regulatory environment for blockchain is constantly evolving, with different jurisdictions adopting various approaches to govern blockchain activities such as cryptocurrencies, smart contracts, and decentralized applications (dApps). Compliance plays a critical role in the feasibility and long-term success of a project.

Navigating Complex Legal Frameworks: The decentralized and borderless nature of blockchain complicates compliance. For instance, the European Union's General Data Protection Regulation (GDPR) has stringent requirements around user privacy, including the "right to be forgotten," which conflicts with the immutable nature of blockchain. Such contradictions necessitate careful consideration of how to balance regulatory demands with the functionality of the blockchain.

Engaging Legal Experts Early: Involving legal and compliance professionals at the initial stages of the project is essential. Their guidance will ensure that the project adheres to regional laws, preventing costly delays or legal complications. Whether it's ensuring that the project complies with anti-money laundering (AML) regulations or addressing tax implications, early legal intervention can safeguard the project from regulatory hurdles.

Consider these regulatory questions:

- Does the blockchain application deal with personal data, and how will it comply with data protection laws?

- Which country or region's laws will the project be subject to, and are there any specific licensing requirements?

- How will smart contracts be regulated under local contract laws?

3. Security and Privacy Concerns

Although blockchain technology offers robust security features, blockchain projects must contend with additional layers of security concerns, especially when interacting with external systems or developing smart contracts.

Smart Contract Vulnerabilities: Smart contracts are self-executing contracts coded directly onto the blockchain, offering automated enforcement of agreements. However, bugs or vulnerabilities within the code can expose the project to attacks. Notable security breaches, such as the DAO hack in Ethereum, underscore the importance of thorough smart contract audits. Engaging blockchain security firms to conduct code audits can mitigate these risks by identifying potential exploits.

Private Key Management: In blockchain ecosystems, users control access to their assets via private keys. Ensuring that end users have secure key management solutions—whether through hardware wallets, multi-signature wallets, or trusted custodians—is vital. Loss or theft of private keys equates to a permanent loss of control over the associated assets, so robust key management is a key aspect of any project.

Critical security steps to consider:

- Conducting regular security audits of smart contracts and the overall blockchain infrastructure.

- Educating users on secure key management practices to prevent unauthorized access and theft.

- Implementing multi-signature approval mechanisms for high-stakes transactions.

4. Integration with Existing Systems

Blockchain solutions often need to integrate seamlessly with an organization's current infrastructure. This process can involve complex customization and a thorough understanding of both blockchain technology and existing systems, such as payment gateways, customer databases, and identity management tools.

Data Interoperability: Fintech projects frequently rely on established databases and data management systems. Introducing blockchain into the mix often requires designing APIs and middleware to ensure interoperability between the blockchain and the organization's existing platforms. This is especially important for industries like finance, where real-time transactions, customer verification, and data reconciliation must be smooth and error-free.

Scalability Concerns: Blockchains, particularly public ones, face inherent scalability limitations. Integrating blockchain with fintech systems may also strain the scalability of both the blockchain and the incumbent systems. Solutions such as Layer 2 scaling protocols, sidechains, or hybrid blockchain architectures should be explored to address this challenge.

Important integration considerations:

- Will blockchain disrupt or complement existing fintech systems, and how will it impact the customer experience?

- What middleware or APIs are necessary to ensure smooth data flow between systems?

- How will the blockchain solution scale as transaction volumes increase?

Each of these considerations highlights the complexities of managing blockchain-based projects. Project managers must not only familiarize themselves with blockchain technology but also proactively address the legal, security, and integration challenges that accompany it. By doing so, they can ensure a smoother implementation and greater long-term success for their blockchain initiatives.

Critical Success Factors in Blockchain Implementation

Successfully implementing a blockchain project, especially within the fintech space, depends on several key factors. These factors not only ensure the technology is executed effectively but also ensure that the project achieves its business goals and meets stakeholder expectations. Let's probe more into the most critical success factors for blockchain implementation.

1. Clearly Defined Use Cases

A clearly defined use case is one of the most crucial factors in ensuring blockchain implementation succeeds. Not all problems require blockchain technology, and using blockchain where it is unnecessary can waste resources and complicate processes.

Problem Identification: The project must address a clear problem that blockchain is uniquely positioned to solve. Whether it's decentralization, enhanced security, or immutability, the chosen blockchain solution must demonstrate why other traditional technologies cannot address the issue as efficiently.

Example: Consider a fintech company developing a blockchain-based identity verification system. The use case must outline why blockchain is necessary—perhaps due to decentralized control, immutable records, or heightened security for storing personal data without relying on a central authority.

Validation: To ensure resources are not wasted, the use case must be well-researched, validated, and aligned with market needs, technical feasibility, and competitor analysis.

2. Strong Collaboration Between Stakeholders

Blockchain projects often span multiple departments and involve a wide range of stakeholders, including developers, business leaders, regulators, and end-users.

Cross-Functional Teams: Success relies on building cross-functional teams with a shared understanding of both the technology and the business requirements. Project managers will need to act as intermediaries between technical developers and non-technical stakeholders to align on goals and expectations.

Communication Channels: Regular meetings, status updates, and shared tools (such as project management software) facilitate continuous collaboration and ensure stakeholders are updated on progress and challenges.

Alignment: Ensuring that business leaders and technical teams are aligned on goals helps avoid miscommunication, delays, and scope creep.

3. Scalability and Performance

Scalability remains one of the key challenges for blockchain projects, especially in the fintech sector, where speed and efficiency are paramount.

Layer-2 Solutions: Technologies such as Layer-2 solutions (rollups, sidechains, etc.) are often used to enhance performance. Layer-2 solutions operate on top of the main blockchain, processing transactions faster and at lower costs.

Blockchain Protocol Choice: Selecting the right blockchain protocol for the project's needs is critical. For example, platforms like Solana and Avalanche, known for their high transaction throughput, are better suited for applications requiring speed and scalability compared to Ethereum, which faces congestion issues.

4. Regulatory Compliance and Legal Considerations

Regulatory compliance plays a significant role in determining the success or failure of blockchain projects, particularly in the fintech sector.

Early Legal Involvement: Involving legal experts early on ensures that the project adheres to all regional and international laws, including those related to data privacy, cryptocurrencies, and financial services.

Regulatory Flexibility: Given the rapidly evolving regulatory landscape, blockchain projects need to remain agile. Project plans must incorporate the flexibility to adjust to changing regulations without affecting the overall timeline or budget.

5. User Experience (UX) and Adoption

Although blockchain offers technical advantages, it can be challenging for non-technical users to understand. A smooth, intuitive user experience is essential for widespread adoption.

Simplification: The complexity of blockchain technology should be hidden from the end-user. Implementing user-friendly interfaces and solutions like hardware wallets or custodial services can make the user experience seamless.

Education and Onboarding: Educating users about blockchain technology through tutorials, user support, and onboarding processes enhances adoption. Projects that invest in education and customer engagement will likely experience higher success rates.

6. Security Measures and Best Practices

Security is of utmost importance for any blockchain project, particularly in fintech, where the potential for financial loss is significant.

Smart Contract Security: Smart contracts are self-executing pieces of code that need to be rigorously audited. Regular security audits, bug bounty programs, and collaboration with blockchain security experts help minimize vulnerabilities.

Private Key Management: Ensuring users have secure and user-friendly key management solutions, such as multi-signature wallets or hardware wallets, can prevent unauthorized access and potential losses.

7. Continuous Testing and Iteration

Ongoing testing and iteration are key to identifying issues early and improving project outcomes. This agile approach also helps adapt to changing market demands or technical challenges.

Pilot Testing: Running pilot tests with a small group of users can provide early feedback on both functionality and usability, which allows the project to refine before a broader launch.

Iterative Development: Adopting agile development methodologies allows blockchain projects to evolve based on user needs and feedback, ensuring the product remains competitive and efficient.

8. Integration with Legacy Systems

Many fintech organizations operate on legacy systems that are decades old. Integrating blockchain into these existing systems can be complex but is essential for blockchain's success in established industries.

APIs and Middleware: To bridge the gap between blockchain networks and traditional financial systems, APIs and middleware solutions are essential. These tools help ensure smooth communication between blockchain-based systems and legacy infrastructure.

Interoperability: Interoperability between various blockchain networks and legacy systems allows for seamless data exchange. Ensuring smooth interoperability is crucial when multiple blockchains or traditional systems are involved.

Successfully managing these factors requires a thoughtful, strategic approach. By considering both the technical and business aspects, blockchain projects in the fintech space are more likely to meet their objectives, satisfy stakeholders, and provide innovative solutions for real-world problems.

Implementing blockchain technology in the fintech sector demands a comprehensive and well-structured approach to project management. Success hinges on several key factors, including a clear understanding of the project's objectives, strong collaboration among stakeholders, adherence to regulatory requirements, and the ability to adapt to both technological advancements and market dynamics.

By prioritizing clearly defined use cases and fostering cross-functional teamwork, fintech organizations can align their efforts and resources effectively. Ensuring regulatory compliance from the outset helps mitigate legal risks and builds trust with users. Additionally, focusing on user experience and security measures not only enhances adoption but also safeguards assets, ultimately driving success in a competitive landscape.

By embracing these core project management strategies, fintech companies can effectively leverage blockchain technology to deliver innovative, secure, and efficient solutions that meet the evolving needs of the market. As the fintech industry continues to transform, those who master these implementation factors will position themselves at the forefront of this technological revolution, paving the way for a future driven by blockchain innovation.

CHAPTER 3: Blockchain Use Cases in Fintech

As already proved in the earlier part of this book, blockchain technology is rapidly becoming a crucial part of the financial technology (Fintech) landscape, transforming how traditional financial systems operate. This chapter looks at how blockchain is used in various Fintech areas, focusing on its ability to improve security, increase efficiency, and provide more transparency. Whether you're just starting to learn about blockchain or want to understand how it works, this chapter will show you some of its most important uses in finance.

Payments and Remittances

One of the most transformative applications of blockchain technology is in the area of payments and remittances. Traditionally, sending money across borders is not only slow but also riddled with high fees and unnecessary complications. For millions of people around the world—especially those who send remittances to their families—navigating the old system means dealing with long wait times, currency conversions, and intermediaries siphoning off fees at each step.

Blockchain is now rewriting this narrative, bringing exceptional speed, cost-efficiency, and transparency to the global payments terrain.

The Problem with Traditional Cross-Border Payments

Imagine sending money from New York to a relative in the Philippines. You initiate the transfer through your bank, but between correspondent banks, currency conversion, and processing delays, your relative might not receive the money for days—and with less in their hand than you initially intended. Hidden fees, slow processing times, and reliance on multiple intermediaries make the process frustratingly inefficient, especially for those who depend on timely remittances.

This is where blockchain steps in to pull down these pain points, offering a radically different approach.

How Blockchain Revolutionizes Payments

Basically, blockchain simplifies cross-border payments by removing the need for intermediaries, such as correspondent banks or money transfer services. Instead of going through several third parties, transactions occur directly between sender and recipient on a decentralized, peer-to-peer network. Each transaction is verified by a network of computers (nodes), which reach consensus, ensuring the authenticity of the transfer.

Once verified, the transaction is permanently recorded on a public ledger, creating a transparent, immutable record accessible to all participants. This decentralized verification eliminates the need for central authorities to process payments, drastically reducing both the time and cost associated with international money transfers.

Key Mechanisms at Play:

- Distributed Ledger: A transparent, real-time record of transactions available to all network participants.

- Consensus Algorithms: Mechanisms (such as Proof of Work or Proof of Stake) ensure that transactions are verified and agreed upon by a majority of the network.

- Cryptographic Security: Advanced cryptographic techniques secure transactions, making blockchain highly resistant to fraud and tampering.

The Core Benefits of Blockchain in Payments

Lightning-Fast Speed: Traditional international payments can take up to 5 business days to clear, especially when different banking systems and regulations are involved. Blockchain-based payments, by contrast, can be completed in minutes, regardless of geographical distance or banking hours. This near-instantaneous processing is a game-changer for individuals and businesses alike.

Drastically Lower Costs: One of the biggest burdens of sending money internationally is the high transaction fees. Banks, payment processors, and currency conversion services all take their cut. Blockchain cuts out the middlemen, significantly lowering transaction costs, making it particularly attractive for those who rely on remittances.

Enhanced Security: Blockchain's cryptographic foundations provide a level of security unmatched by traditional payment systems. The data within each block is encrypted and linked to previous blocks, making it nearly impossible to alter past transactions. This offers an extra layer of protection against fraud and unauthorized tampering.

Financial Inclusion: Perhaps one of the most far-reaching impacts of blockchain in payments is its potential to provide financial services to billions of unbanked individuals. Many people in developing regions lack access to traditional banking, either due to geographical barriers or high costs. With blockchain, anyone with an internet connection and a smartphone can participate in the global economy, sending and receiving funds securely.

Case Study: Ripple—The Pioneer of Blockchain Payments

A key example of blockchain's power in remittances is Ripple, a real-time gross settlement system designed to enable instant, low-cost international payments. Launched in 2012, Ripple has quickly become a cornerstone of blockchain-based cross-border payment solutions.

Unlike Bitcoin or Ethereum, Ripple focuses on improving existing financial infrastructure rather than replacing it. Its native cryptocurrency, XRP, is used as a bridge between different fiat currencies, allowing banks and financial institutions to settle transactions instantly without the need for costly intermediary exchanges.

Through partnerships with over 300 financial institutions worldwide, Ripple's blockchain-based solution has dramatically reduced the cost and time of sending money across borders. In fact, many major financial institutions, including Santander and American Express, use Ripple's technology to provide faster, more affordable services to their customers. Ripple's network offers a compelling alternative to the outdated SWIFT system, which has dominated international banking for decades but is known for being slow and expensive.

A Glimpse Into the Future

The use of blockchain in payments is just the beginning. As the technology matures, blockchain could play an even larger role in the future of global finance. For example, central bank digital currencies (CBDCs) are currently being explored by various nations, which could further streamline cross-border payments. Decentralized finance (DeFi) is also making strides by offering blockchain-based financial services, including loans, savings, and investments, without the need for traditional banks.

The transformative potential of blockchain in payments and remittances lies in its ability to transcend borders, reduce costs, and extend financial services to underserved populations. As the world becomes more interconnected and the demand for faster, cheaper payments grows, blockchain is positioned to become the backbone of the global financial system, reshaping how we move money across borders forever.

Decentralized Finance (DeFi)

Decentralized finance, or DeFi, is at the forefront of a seismic shift in how financial services are delivered and accessed. By leveraging blockchain technology, DeFi aims to dismantle traditional financial systems, offering open, transparent, and permissionless alternatives to services typically controlled by banks, brokers, and other financial intermediaries. In a period where the current financial system is often criticized for being slow, expensive, and exclusive, DeFi offers a radically different approach.

What is DeFi?

DeFi encompasses a broad ecosystem of decentralized applications (DApps) that mimic traditional financial services like lending, borrowing, trading, saving, and earning interest —but without a central authority. Instead of relying on banks or financial institutions, DeFi platforms operate on blockchain networks such as Ethereum, using smart contracts to automate and manage transactions.

Smart contracts are self-executing contracts where the terms of the agreement are written directly into code. This eliminates the need for intermediaries, as the contract automatically triggers actions when predefined conditions are met. For example, a smart contract could automatically transfer funds between two parties once certain conditions, such as loan repayment or an interest rate, are satisfied.

By cutting out the middlemen and using transparent code, DeFi empowers individuals to have complete control over their assets, financial agreements, and transactions.

Core Features of DeFi

Decentralization: Unlike traditional finance, where banks and institutions control transactions, DeFi operates on decentralized blockchain networks, where transactions are processed and verified by a distributed network of computers (nodes). This means there is no single point of control or failure.

Interoperability: DeFi platforms are often designed to interact seamlessly with one another, creating a network of interconnected financial services that users can switch between without friction. This composability allows developers to build complex financial products by stacking multiple services on top of each other.

Transparency and Trustlessness: All transactions on DeFi platforms are publicly recorded on the blockchain, ensuring transparency and accountability. Anyone can audit these transactions in real time, eliminating the need for blind trust in financial intermediaries. Moreover, DeFi protocols are "trustless," meaning users don't need to trust a central authority to manage their funds; they trust the code instead.

Programmability: DeFi applications (DApps) leverage smart contracts to create programmable financial instruments. This allows for the creation of advanced financial products, such as automated loans, insurance policies, derivatives, and decentralized exchanges (DEXs), that can be customized to meet specific needs.

Global Accessibility: Unlike traditional financial systems that require documentation, credit checks, and local infrastructure, DeFi is accessible to anyone with an internet connection. This opens up financial opportunities to millions of unbanked and underbanked individuals around the world, offering services that were previously out of reach.

How DeFi Works: Key Financial Services

DeFi replicates many traditional financial services but with the added benefits of decentralization, automation, and transparency. Here's a closer look at some of the core financial applications within DeFi:

Lending and Borrowing: DeFi protocols allow users to lend their digital assets to others and earn interest, or borrow assets by using their own holdings as collateral. Unlike traditional banking, where a central institution approves loans, DeFi loans are handled through smart contracts that automatically manage interest rates and collateral levels.

Borrowers must over-collateralize their loans (i.e., provide more value in collateral than the amount borrowed) to account for the volatility of cryptocurrencies. If the value of the collateral falls below a certain threshold, the smart contract will automatically liquidate the collateral to protect the lender, ensuring that loans remain secure.

- **Example:** Aave, a popular DeFi lending protocol, allows users to earn interest on deposits or borrow assets with over-collateralized loans. Users deposit funds into Aave's liquidity pool, and the protocol issues loans using these pooled assets. Interest rates are algorithmically determined based on the supply and demand of the assets in the pool.

Decentralized Exchanges (DEXs): Traditional exchanges rely on central operators to facilitate trading between users. DEXs, on the other hand, allow users to trade directly with one another, using liquidity pools and smart contracts to facilitate transactions. DEXs remove the need for a central authority, giving users full control over their funds.

- **Example:** Uniswap is one of the largest DEXs in the DeFi space. It uses an automated market-making (AMM) model, where users provide liquidity to pools by depositing their assets, and traders can exchange assets directly with these pools. In return, liquidity providers earn fees from the trades facilitated by the pool.

Yield Farming and Liquidity Mining: Yield farming refers to the practice of earning additional cryptocurrency by providing liquidity to DeFi platforms. Users can "stake" their crypto in liquidity pools, and in exchange, they receive rewards, often in the form of the platform's native token. This incentivizes users to lock up their assets, ensuring liquidity for other users on the platform.

- **Example:** Yearn Finance is a DeFi protocol that automates yield farming strategies. It helps users maximize returns by automatically shifting their funds between different yield-generating platforms to capture the best interest rates.

Stablecoins: Cryptocurrencies are known for their volatility, which can make them unsuitable for everyday transactions. Stablecoins, which are pegged to traditional assets like the U.S. dollar or gold, offer a solution. DeFi platforms often use stablecoins for trading, lending, and borrowing because they provide price stability while maintaining the benefits of blockchain technology.

- **Example:** DAI, a decentralized stablecoin issued by the MakerDAO protocol, is pegged to the U.S. dollar but backed by cryptocurrency collateral. Unlike centralized stablecoins like Tether, which are backed by fiat reserves, DAI maintains its peg through over-collateralization and smart contract governance.

Decentralized Insurance: DeFi is also transforming the insurance industry. With decentralized insurance platforms, users can pool funds to cover specific risks, and smart contracts automate the claims process, reducing the potential for disputes and fraud. Policies can be customized and issued without the need for traditional insurance companies.

- **Example:** Nexus Mutual is a decentralized insurance platform that allows users to buy coverage against smart contract failures or exchange hacks. The platform is governed by a decentralized autonomous organization (DAO), where participants vote on claims and the management of the insurance pool.

The Benefits of DeFi

Financial Inclusion: DeFi opens the doors to financial services for individuals who are excluded from traditional banking systems, particularly in developing countries. People can access lending, borrowing, and trading services without needing a credit score, bank account, or financial history.

Transparency and Auditability: Every transaction on a DeFi platform is publicly recorded on the blockchain, making financial operations fully transparent. Users can audit transactions and even review the code behind the smart contracts, reducing the potential for corruption or hidden fees.

Intermediary-Free Services: By eliminating middlemen such as banks or brokers, DeFi allows for direct peer-to-peer transactions. This not only speeds up transactions but also reduces fees, making financial services more affordable.

Programmability: The use of smart contracts enables highly customizable and programmable financial products. From automated loans to derivative products, DeFi introduces an unprecedented level of flexibility in creating financial services.

Real-World Example: Compound—Pioneering Decentralized Lending

Compound is a leading DeFi platform that enables users to lend and borrow cryptocurrencies in a decentralized manner. It operates using liquidity pools, where users deposit their digital assets, earning interest in the process. Borrowers can take out loans from these pools by providing collateral in the form of other cryptocurrencies.

One of Compound's key innovations is the use of algorithmically determined interest rates, which automatically adjust based on the supply and demand of each asset. For example, if there is high demand for borrowing a particular asset, the interest rate for that asset increases, incentivizing more users to deposit their assets into the pool.

Compound's use of smart contracts ensures that the lending process is fully automated, fair, and transparent. Lenders are guaranteed to receive their interest, and borrowers are required to maintain their collateral above a certain threshold. If the value of the collateral drops too low, the smart contract liquidates the borrower's assets to protect the lender, eliminating the need for a third party to manage risk.

Risks and Challenges of DeFi

While the potential of DeFi is immense, it is not without risks. Some of the key challenges facing DeFi include:

Smart Contract Vulnerabilities: DeFi platforms rely on code, which means that bugs or vulnerabilities in smart contracts can lead to significant losses. Hacks and exploits have already resulted in millions of dollars in lost funds.

Market Volatility: Many DeFi platforms require users to over-collateralize their loans due to the volatility of cryptocurrencies. Sudden market crashes can lead to liquidation events, where users lose their collateral.

Regulatory Uncertainty: As DeFi grows, it is attracting more attention from regulators. Governments are still figuring out how to regulate decentralized platforms, and future regulations could impact the growth and functionality of DeFi services.

(DeFi) A New Financial Frontier

DeFi has already transformed the way people think about finance, but its potential is far from fully realized. As the ecosystem matures, we can expect to see increased integration with other blockchain technologies, such as tokenized real-world assets (e.g., real estate or commodities) and central bank digital currencies (CBDCs). The rise of decentralized autonomous organizations (DAOs) will also bring new governance structures to DeFi platforms, allowing for more democratic decision-making.

Ultimately, DeFi has the potential to reshape the entire global financial landscape, making it more efficient, inclusive, and transparent. As it continues to evolve, decentralized finance may become the backbone of a new, decentralized global economy.

Know Your Customer (KYC) and Anti-Money Laundering (AML) Processes

In today's global financial ecosystem, compliance with **Know Your Customer (KYC)** and **Anti-Money Laundering (AML)** regulations is critical for preventing illicit activities such as money laundering, fraud, and terrorism financing. However, traditional methods of KYC and AML are often seen as cumbersome, time-consuming, and costly for financial institutions and customers alike. Blockchain technology offers a way to revolutionize these processes by making them more efficient, secure, and customer-friendly.

What are KYC and AML?

Know Your Customer (KYC) refers to the process that financial institutions and businesses use to verify the identity of their clients. This includes gathering personal information, such as name, address, and government-issued identification, to ensure that customers are who they say they are. The goal of KYC is to prevent fraud, identity theft, and financial crimes by ensuring that financial services are not used for illicit purposes.

Anti-Money Laundering (AML) involves a broader set of laws, regulations, and procedures that financial institutions must follow to detect and prevent illegal money laundering activities. Money laundering is the process of making large sums of money generated by criminal activity (such as drug trafficking, fraud, or terrorism financing) appear to be earned legally. AML practices aim to trace the origin of funds and ensure that they are not linked to illegal activities.

Both KYC and AML are legally required in most jurisdictions, and failure to comply can result in heavy penalties for financial institutions, including fines, sanctions, or loss of licenses. These regulations, while essential, have traditionally been resource-intensive, involving lengthy paperwork, manual verification processes, and a lack of interoperability between systems.

The Problem with Traditional KYC and AML Processes

Traditional KYC and AML processes suffer from several key inefficiencies:

Lengthy and Costly Procedures: Onboarding a new customer can take days or even weeks, as financial institutions must manually verify documents, run background checks, and ensure compliance with regulatory frameworks. This not only frustrates customers but also leads to high operational costs for businesses.

Data Duplication and Silos: Many financial institutions rely on their own internal databases for customer verification, leading to a situation where customers must repeatedly submit the same information across different institutions. This not only increases the time and effort required for verification but also leads to data silos, where institutions do not share identity information with one another.

Security Vulnerabilities: Storing sensitive customer information on centralized servers makes this data vulnerable to hacking, theft, and breaches. Once a centralized database is compromised, all customer data stored within it is at risk.

Customer Privacy Concerns: Traditional KYC processes often involve sharing personal information across multiple platforms, raising concerns about how much control customers have over their personal data and who has access to it.

How Blockchain Enhances KYC and AML Processes

Blockchain technology offers a more efficient, secure, and privacy-preserving way to handle KYC and AML processes. By capitalizing on decentralized, immutable ledgers and smart contracts, blockchain can streamline identity verification, reduce costs, and provide greater control over personal data for both institutions and customers.

Here's how blockchain improves KYC and AML:

1. Decentralized Digital Identities: With blockchain, customers can create **decentralized digital identities**, which are verified once and then reused across multiple financial institutions or service providers. These digital identities are stored on a distributed ledger, which means they are accessible to authorized entities but not controlled by any single organization.

   - How it works: When a customer initially registers their identity on the blockchain, a financial institution (or another trusted entity) verifies their information and records it on the blockchain in an encrypted form. Once verified, this digital identity can be reused across multiple platforms without the need for repeated verification, speeding up the onboarding process.

2. Immutable Records and Audits: Blockchain's most significant advantage lies in its immutability. Once a record is written on the blockchain, it cannot be altered or tampered with, ensuring that all KYC and AML checks are secure, transparent, and traceable. This immutability allows for seamless auditing and regulatory compliance without the need for manual record-keeping.

   - How it works: Every time a customer's identity is verified, the verification is logged as a transaction on the blockchain. Auditors and regulatory bodies can review these transactions without needing to go through piles of paperwork, significantly reducing the time and effort required for audits.

3. Interoperability and Data Sharing: One of the most significant inefficiencies in traditional KYC processes is that institutions rarely share customer identity data with one another. Blockchain solves this issue by enabling **secure data sharing** between multiple entities. Once a customer's identity is verified on the blockchain, it can be accessed (with consent) by other organizations, reducing the need for duplicate verification.

- **How it works:** When a financial institution verifies a customer's identity, other institutions can view and confirm the customer's information through the blockchain without requiring a re-verification process. This interoperability is facilitated through **permissioned blockchains** or **public blockchains** with privacy controls, ensuring that only authorized parties have access to personal data.

4. Smart Contracts for Automation: Smart contractsself-executing contracts with the terms of the agreement directly written into code—can automate KYC and AML processes. They can trigger specific actions, such as automatic reporting of suspicious activity or alerting regulators when a transaction exceeds certain thresholds.

- **How it works:** For example, a smart contract could be programmed to freeze accounts or report transactions that exceed a specific limit without human intervention. This automation allows for real-time compliance with AML regulations, reducing the risk of human error and speeding up the process of identifying illicit activities.

5. Data Security and Privacy: Blockchain uses advanced cryptographic techniques to protect personal information. With **zero-knowledge proofs** (a cryptographic method where one party can prove to another that they know a value without conveying any information apart from the fact that they know it), customers can verify their identity without revealing sensitive personal information. This ensures compliance with KYC and AML regulations while preserving user privacy.

- **How it works:** Instead of sharing a customer's full personal details, only a cryptographic proof of their identity is shared on the blockchain, ensuring that their sensitive information remains private while still being compliant with regulatory requirements.

Key Benefits of Blockchain for KYC and AML

1. Increased Efficiency: Blockchain dramatically reduces the time required to verify customer identities and run AML checks. What used to take days or weeks can now be done in minutes or hours. By having a single verified identity on the blockchain, customers can onboard multiple services without needing to go through repetitive identity checks.

2. Improved Security: Personal data stored on the blockchain is encrypted and decentralized, significantly reducing the risk of data breaches compared to centralized databases. Each identity verification process is logged immutably, providing a secure, transparent history of identity checks.

3. Reduced Costs: Automating KYC and AML processes through blockchain reduces the need for manual oversight, paperwork, and third-party verification services. Financial institutions can save on operational costs while improving the customer experience with faster onboarding.

4. Customer Privacy and Control: With blockchain, customers have more control over their personal data. They decide who has access to their identity and for how long. This is in contrast to traditional methods, where customers must hand over their data to multiple third parties with little transparency over how it is used.

Real-World Example: Civic – Decentralized Identity Verification

Civic is one of the leading blockchain-based platforms focused on decentralized identity verification. The Civic platform allows users to create and manage their digital identity securely on the blockchain. Once their identity is verified, they can use it to access multiple services without needing to go through KYC checks repeatedly.

- How Civic works: Users upload their personal information and identification documents to the Civic app. Civic verifies their identity and stores the information on the blockchain in an encrypted format. When users need to verify their identity for another service (e.g., opening a bank account, or accessing a government service), they can share their pre-verified information with the service provider securely, without revealing unnecessary details.

For businesses, Civic simplifies KYC compliance by providing verified identities, reducing the time and cost of onboarding customers. Meanwhile, users retain control over their identity, deciding what information to share and with whom.

The Future of KYC and AML with Blockchain

As blockchain technology evolves, its impact on KYC and AML processes will likely grow. In the near future, we may see:

Global KYC Platforms: With blockchain, it's possible to create a global, interoperable KYC platform where users can create a single digital identity accepted by multiple institutions across jurisdictions, reducing compliance burdens.

Decentralized Compliance: The rise of decentralized autonomous organizations (DAOs) could lead to decentralized compliance systems, where smart contracts automatically enforce KYC and AML requirements without human oversight.

AI-Powered Compliance: Combining blockchain with artificial intelligence (AI) could enable real-time monitoring and reporting of suspicious transactions, further enhancing compliance with AML regulations.

Tokenization of Assets

Tokenization is rapidly becoming one of the most transformative applications of blockchain technology, offering a new way to represent ownership of real-world and digital assets on a distributed ledger. By converting physical assets into **blockchain-based tokens**, tokenization not only redefines how ownership is recorded and transferred but also opens up entirely new investment opportunities.

Whether it's real estate, commodities, fine art, or even intellectual property, the process of tokenization is reshaping traditional financial markets and democratizing access to previously inaccessible assets. Tokenized assets can be bought, sold, or traded more efficiently, with a potential to transform industries by unlocking liquidity, reducing costs, and enhancing transparency.

What is Tokenization?

Tokenization refers to the process of creating a digital representation—or token—of an asset on a blockchain. These tokens represent ownership or a stake in the underlying asset, whether it's tangible (such as real estate or commodities) or intangible (such as intellectual property or digital art).

Here's a simple breakdown:

1. The Asset: The asset being tokenized could be anything from real estate, fine art, and stocks to digital goods like intellectual property, or even more abstract concepts such as carbon credits or loyalty points.

2. The Token: A **token** is a digital unit that represents a specific portion of the asset. Depending on how the asset is tokenized, each token could represent a fractional share of the asset or the entire asset.

3. The Blockchain: The token is issued on a blockchain, which acts as the public ledger to store, record, and track transactions involving the token. The blockchain's decentralized nature ensures that ownership and transaction history are transparent and immutable.

How Tokenization Works

Issuance: The asset owner or custodian creates digital tokens that represent ownership in the underlying asset. These tokens are issued on a blockchain, which could be a public blockchain (e.g., Ethereum) or a private/permissioned blockchain, depending on the application.

Ownership Representation: Each token corresponds to a portion of the asset's value. For example, if a building is worth $1 million and the owner issues 100,000 tokens, each token would represent 0.001% of the building's value.

Trading: Once issued, these tokens can be traded on a secondary market, just like stocks. Investors can buy and sell tokens, representing fractional ownership in the asset, on blockchain platforms or decentralized exchanges (DEXs).

Smart Contracts: Smart contracts are often embedded within the tokens to govern the rules for transactions and ownership. These contracts automatically enforce terms, such as transferring dividends, handling interest payments, or triggering the transfer of ownership based on certain conditions.

Key Benefits of Tokenization

Tokenization offers several groundbreaking benefits that address some of the limitations of traditional finance, especially when it comes to the transfer and management of high-value or illiquid assets. These benefits are particularly important for fintech applications and blockchain-based ecosystems.

1. Increased Liquidity: One of the most significant advantages of tokenization is liquidity. Traditionally, assets like real estate, fine art, or private equity are considered illiquid—they cannot easily be sold or converted to cash. Tokenization changes this by enabling these assets to be divided into smaller, tradeable tokens that can be easily bought and sold on secondary markets.

- **How it works:** In traditional real estate, for example, selling a property can take months or even years due to the need for legal paperwork, inspections, and title transfers. However, when real estate is tokenized, individual tokens representing portions of the property can be sold almost instantly on a blockchain marketplace. This creates liquidity in an otherwise illiquid market by allowing a portion of the property to be sold without needing to sell the entire asset.

2. Fractional Ownership: Another key advantage is **fractional ownership**. High-value assets such as luxury real estate, fine art, or rare commodities are typically out of reach for the average investor due to their high cost of entry. Tokenization enables these assets to be split into smaller units, giving everyday investors the ability to own a portion of the asset.

- **How it works:** Imagine a luxury painting worth $10 million. Traditionally, only a wealthy individual or institution would be able to buy it. However, if this painting is tokenized into 10,000 tokens, each token could represent 0.01% of the painting's value. This enables a broader range of investors to purchase tokens, providing access to high-value assets that were previously unattainable.

This **democratization** of investment opens up entirely new possibilities, allowing individuals to diversify their portfolios by investing in high-value assets with smaller amounts of capital.

3. Transparency and Trust: Because blockchain is inherently transparent, tokenization enhances trust by providing an immutable, transparent record of ownership, transactions, and the asset's history. Once an asset is tokenized, every transaction involving that asset is recorded on the blockchain, allowing for easy verification of who owns what and when.

- **How it works:** For example, if a tokenized real estate property is sold, the blockchain would store the full history of the property's ownership, offering complete transparency for buyers, sellers, and regulators. This eliminates the need for lengthy due diligence processes, such as verifying titles, because the blockchain provides an irrefutable record.

4. Reduced Costs and Improved Efficiency: Tokenization also reduces transaction costs by eliminating intermediaries. Traditional asset transactions often require numerous middlemen—such as brokers, escrow agents, and lawyers —which increases both time and costs. Blockchain-based tokenization enables peer-to-peer transactions, facilitated by smart contracts, that cut out intermediaries and streamline the process.

- **How it works**: For example, in real estate transactions, instead of going through a broker, the seller can transfer tokens directly to the buyer on a blockchain marketplace, and a smart contract can automatically handle the transfer of ownership. This minimizes fees, speeds up transactions, and makes the entire process more efficient.

Real-World Example: Real Estate Tokenization

One of the most promising applications of tokenization is in **real estate**. Traditionally, real estate investments have been restricted to high-net-worth individuals or institutions, and real estate markets are typically illiquid. Tokenization solves both of these problems by allowing fractional ownership and increasing liquidity.

RealT: RealT is a blockchain-based platform that allows investors to buy fractional ownership in real estate properties. Each property is represented by tokens on the blockchain, and these tokens can be bought, sold, or traded just like any other digital asset. Investors receive **rental income** proportional to their token ownership, and they can also benefit from the property's appreciation over time.

  - **How it works:** Imagine a property worth $1 million. RealT tokenizes the property by issuing 10,000 tokens, with each token representing a fractional share of the property. Investors can purchase these tokens for as little as $100, gaining a share of the property's rental income and potential value appreciation. The tokens can also be traded on secondary markets, providing liquidity that traditional real estate investments typically lack.

This innovative approach democratizes real estate investment**, enabling more people to participate in the market while also making it easier to sell or transfer ownership through blockchain platforms.

Tokenization Beyond Real Estate

While real estate is a highly visible use case for tokenization, other sectors are beginning to embrace this technology as well:

Art and Collectibles: Platforms like **Maecenas** allow for the tokenization of high-value art pieces, enabling fractional ownership of artworks and collectibles. Investors can own a portion of rare paintings, sculptures, or even NFTs (non-fungible tokens), which are unique digital assets stored on the blockchain.

Commodities: Tokenization is also being applied to commodities like gold, silver, and oil. For instance, **Tether Gold** (XAUT) is a digital token backed by physical gold reserves, enabling investors to own gold in a digital format that can be easily traded.

Intellectual Property: Creative works, patents, and intellectual property can also be tokenized. By issuing tokens that represent ownership or licensing rights, creators can monetize their work more efficiently, while buyers can trade these rights on blockchain platforms.

Challenges and Considerations

While tokenization offers tremendous potential, several challenges must be addressed for widespread adoption:

Regulatory Compliance: Tokenizing assets—especially those tied to real-world physical assets like real estate or commodities—requires navigating complex regulatory frameworks. Different jurisdictions have varying rules around securities, ownership, and taxation, making compliance a critical issue for tokenization platforms.

Asset Custodianship: The relationship between the digital token and the real-world asset must be carefully managed. For example, who is responsible for maintaining or managing a physical property that has been tokenized? There needs to be a robust framework for ensuring that the underlying asset continues to function as expected.

Market Adoption: Tokenization is still a relatively new concept, and convincing traditional investors and institutions to embrace blockchain-based asset ownership may take time. Market education and trust-building are essential to achieving broader adoption.

The Future of Tokenization

As blockchain technology continues to evolve, the tokenization of assets has the potential to transform entire industries by creating more liquid, accessible, and efficient markets. In the near future, we can expect to see:

Tokenized Stock Exchanges: Stock exchanges may begin issuing tokenized versions of shares, allowing for real-time trading, 24/7 markets, and cross-border investments without the need for intermediaries.

Tokenized Carbon Credits: As sustainability becomes a growing priority, we may see the tokenization of carbon credits and other environmental assets, allowing for more transparent and efficient markets for trading carbon offsets.

Global Asset Markets: Tokenization could pave the way for a truly global marketplace for all kinds of assets, breaking down barriers between different countries and creating an interconnected financial ecosystem.

Conclusion

The integration of **blockchain technology** into the fintech landscape is not merely an incremental improvement; it represents a profound **overhaul** in how financial services operate. By fundamentally altering the mechanics of transactions, data management, and trust, blockchain has the capability to redefine financial systems and reshape the global economy.

From enhancing traditional payment systems and enabling **decentralized finance (DeFi)** to improving compliance through streamlined **KYC** and **AML** processes, the applications of blockchain technology are diverse and extensive. This transformative technology empowers individuals by providing greater access to financial services, reducing costs, and enhancing transparency and security. As we navigate the complexities of this new digital frontier, the potential benefits of blockchain extend beyond mere efficiency; they promise to democratize finance, making it more inclusive and accessible to populations previously marginalized by traditional banking systems.

As fintech innovators continue to explore the capabilities of blockchain, collaboration between technology providers, financial institutions, and regulatory bodies will be crucial in crafting frameworks that foster innovation while safeguarding users.

As we look to the future, it is essential to remain vigilant and adaptable. The evolving landscape of blockchain in fintech holds exciting possibilities, including the tokenization of assets, the emergence of digital currencies, and the potential for completely new financial instruments. Embracing this technology could lead to a more resilient financial system, better equipped to respond to the needs of a rapidly changing world.

Finally, the journey of integrating blockchain into financial services is just beginning. As stakeholders across the financial ecosystem explore the implications and opportunities presented by this groundbreaking technology, we stand at the cusp of a financial revolution that could profoundly impact how we interact with money, assets, and each other. Understanding and embracing these changes will be crucial for leveraging the full potential of blockchain technology to create a more efficient, transparent, and equitable financial landscape for all.

CHAPTER 4: Risk Management in Blockchain Projects

Risk management in blockchain projects is a systematic approach to identifying, assessing, and mitigating risks that can impact project outcomes. Given the complexity and novelty of blockchain technology, risk management is essential to ensure that projects remain on track, meet regulatory requirements, and ultimately achieve their objectives. In the fintech sector, where security, reliability, and compliance are paramount, effective risk management is crucial for building trust with users and stakeholders.

Importance of Risk Management

Enhancing Project Success

Effective risk management enables project managers to foresee potential obstacles and develop strategies to address them, which significantly increases the chances of project success.

Building Stakeholder Confidence

By demonstrating a thorough understanding of risks and a proactive approach to managing them, project managers can build confidence among stakeholders, including investors, regulators, and customers. This trust is particularly important in fintech, where data security and compliance are critical.

Compliance with Regulatory Standards

The regulatory landscape for blockchain and fintech is complex and continually evolving. Effective risk management ensures that projects comply with relevant laws and regulations, reducing the risk of legal challenges and penalties.

Protecting Reputation

In the digital age, reputation is invaluable. A single security breach or regulatory failure can have devastating consequences for a project's reputation. Effective risk management helps safeguard against such incidents.

Maximizing Resource Efficiency

By identifying risks early, project managers can allocate resources more effectively, ensuring that time and money are spent on activities that enhance project success rather than on rectifying issues that arise from unmanaged risks.

Key Components of Risk Management in Blockchain Projects

Risk Identification

This involves systematically identifying potential risks associated with blockchain technology and its application in projects. Risks can be technical (e.g., software bugs, scalability issues) or operational (e.g., human error, vendor risks). Techniques for risk identification include brainstorming sessions, expert interviews, and checklists.

Risk Assessment

Once risks are identified, project managers need to assess their potential impact and likelihood. This process often involves qualitative and quantitative analysis. Understanding the severity of each risk helps prioritize them based on their potential impact on project success.

Risk Mitigation

After assessing risks, project managers develop strategies to mitigate them. Mitigation strategies can include:

- Preventive Measures: Implementing coding standards and quality assurance processes to reduce the likelihood of software bugs.

- Contingency Planning: Developing backup plans for critical components to ensure continuity in case of failure.

- Training and Education: Providing ongoing training for team members to minimize human error.

Risk Monitoring

Continuous monitoring of risks is crucial throughout the project lifecycle. Project managers should establish key performance indicators (KPIs) and regularly review risk status to ensure that mitigation strategies are effective and to identify any new risks that may arise.

Risk Communication

Clear communication about risks is essential for fostering a culture of transparency within the project team and among stakeholders. Regularly updating stakeholders on risk status and mitigation efforts helps maintain confidence and support for the project.

Specific Risk Management Strategies for Blockchain Fintech Projects

Addressing Technical Risks

Robust Testing: Implement rigorous testing protocols, including unit testing, integration testing, and penetration testing, to identify and address software vulnerabilities early in the development process.

Scalability Planning: Assess the scalability of the blockchain solution from the outset. This may involve choosing the right consensus mechanism and planning for future growth.

Regulatory Compliance

Stay Informed: Continuously monitor regulatory changes and engage with legal experts to ensure compliance with local and international laws. This includes understanding KYC (Know Your Customer), AML (Anti-Money Laundering), and data protection regulations.

Compliance Framework: Develop a compliance framework that integrates regulatory requirements into project processes and technologies, ensuring that compliance is part of the project lifecycle rather than an afterthought.

Data Privacy and Security

Implement Strong Encryption: Use robust encryption protocols to protect sensitive user data and transactions.

Regular Security Audits: Conduct regular audits and vulnerability assessments to identify potential security weaknesses and rectify them promptly.

Change Management

Develop Change Management Processes: As blockchain technology evolves, projects may need to adapt to new developments. Establish clear processes for managing changes in project scope, technology, or team composition to minimize disruptions.

Vendor Management

Careful Selection of Vendors: Conduct thorough due diligence when selecting vendors and partners. Establish clear contracts that define roles, responsibilities, and expectations regarding security and compliance.

Ongoing Monitoring: Regularly evaluate vendor performance and security practices to ensure they meet project standards.

Identifying Technical and Operational Risks

Understanding Technical Risks

Technical risks can pose significant challenges for project managers overseeing blockchain projects. These risks, if not managed properly, can derail project timelines, budgets, and outcomes. The following outlines key technical risks and their implications for project management and fintech success:

1. Software Bugs and Vulnerabilities

Role of Project Managers: Bugs in the code can lead to unexpected failures that compromise system functionality. For project managers, this means that rigorous testing and quality assurance processes must be prioritized throughout the development lifecycle. This involves setting clear expectations for testing, defining criteria for success, and establishing a feedback loop for continuous improvement.

Implication for Fintech Success: In the fintech sector, where trust and security are paramount, unresolved software vulnerabilities can lead to significant financial losses and reputational damage. A single breach can undermine user confidence and lead to regulatory scrutiny. Project managers play a critical role in fostering a culture of quality assurance, promoting best practices in coding and testing to build and maintain trust with users

2. Scalability Issues

Role of Project Managers: As blockchain projects grow, project managers must plan for scalability from the outset. This includes conducting capacity planning exercises and understanding how increased usage will affect system performance. Failure to anticipate scalability needs can result in performance bottlenecks that compromise user experience and threaten the viability of the project.

Implication for Fintech Success: Scalability is crucial in fintech to accommodate increased transaction volumes and user demands. A project that cannot scale effectively risks losing competitive edge to more agile solutions. Project managers must proactively assess scalability options, such as layer-2 solutions or alternative consensus mechanisms, to ensure the project's long-term success.

3. Integration Challenges

Role of Project Managers: Integrating blockchain technology with legacy systems can be complex and fraught with challenges. Project managers must coordinate between various teams—developers, IT, compliance, and business stakeholders —to ensure that integration efforts align with overall project goals. Clear communication and collaboration are essential in navigating these challenges.

Implication for Fintech Success: Successful integration is vital for operational efficiency and data consistency. When project managers facilitate smooth integration, they enhance the likelihood of project success and user satisfaction. Moreover, the ability to seamlessly connect with existing systems can provide a competitive advantage in the fintech market.

4. Performance and Reliability Risks

Role of Project Managers: Blockchain systems can experience performance issues under heavy loads or due to network failures. Project managers must implement monitoring tools and performance benchmarks to proactively identify and address potential issues.

Implication for Fintech Success: In the fast-paced fintech environment, any downtime or lag in transaction processing can lead to lost opportunities and frustrated users. Ensuring high availability and reliability is crucial for maintaining user trust and satisfaction.

5. Interoperability Risks

Role of Project Managers: With numerous blockchain platforms and protocols in existence, ensuring interoperability between different systems can be challenging. Project managers must advocate for open standards and work closely with stakeholders to establish clear communication channels.

Implication for Fintech Success: Interoperability can drive innovation and enhance user experiences by allowing seamless transactions across platforms. Successful interoperability can lead to greater market adoption and improved competitiveness.

Understanding Operational Risks

Operational risks often stem from the people and processes involved in blockchain projects. These risks can be mitigated through effective project management practices:

1. Human Error

Role on Project Managers: Mistakes made by team members can derail project timelines and outcomes. Project managers must establish clear protocols and provide adequate training to minimize the likelihood of human error. This includes creating a culture of accountability where team members are encouraged to report mistakes and learn from them.

Implication for Fintech Success: In fintech, where accuracy and reliability are critical, human errors can result in significant financial consequences. By implementing rigorous training programs and establishing error-prevention mechanisms, project managers contribute to enhanced project stability and user trust.

2. Insufficient Project Management

Role of Project Managers: Poor project management practices can lead to missed deadlines, budget overruns, and scope creep. Project managers must adopt effective methodologies, such as agile or lean project management, to ensure that projects stay on track and adapt to changing circumstances.

Implication for Fintech Success: Successful fintech projects require timely delivery and adherence to budget constraints. By implementing sound project management practices, project managers can drive successful outcomes, foster stakeholder confidence, and ensure the project meets its strategic objectives.

3. Vendor and Third-Party Risks

Role of Project Managers: Relying on external vendors can introduce risks that project managers need to address through careful selection and ongoing monitoring. Project managers must conduct thorough due diligence when choosing vendors, establishing clear contractual obligations, and maintaining strong communication channels.

Implication for Fintech Success: Vendor failures can lead to disruptions, financial losses, and reputational damage. By effectively managing vendor relationships, project managers help ensure that projects remain on track and deliver value to stakeholders.

4. Communication Gaps

Role of Project Managers: Effective communication is vital for project success. Project managers must facilitate open lines of communication among all stakeholders, ensuring that everyone is aligned on project objectives, timelines, and expectations.

Implication for Fintech Success: Clear communication can prevent misunderstandings and misalignment, leading to smoother project execution and enhanced stakeholder satisfaction. Project managers who prioritize communication create an environment of trust and collaboration that benefits the entire project.

5. Change Management

Role of Project Managers: Implementing new blockchain solutions often involves significant changes to existing processes and systems. Project managers must develop robust change management strategies to guide teams through transitions and ensure that users adapt to new technologies.

Implication for Fintech Success: Effective change management reduces resistance and fosters acceptance of new solutions. By ensuring that users are adequately prepared for changes, project managers enhance the likelihood of successful implementation and adoption.

Effective risk management is crucial for project managers overseeing blockchain projects in the fintech sector. By identifying technical and operational risks and understanding their implications, project managers can navigate the complexities of blockchain technology. Their proactive approach not only safeguards project integrity but also enhances stakeholder confidence and contributes to the overall success of fintech initiatives.

By implementing sound risk management practices, project managers help create resilient projects that can adapt to challenges and capitalize on the transformative potential of blockchain technology. This commitment to managing risks effectively ultimately positions fintech projects for long-term success in an increasingly competitive landscape.

Managing Regulatory Challenges

The regulatory environment surrounding blockchain technology and the fintech sector is complex, dynamic, and often fragmented across jurisdictions. As blockchain projects aim to innovate within the financial services space, they must navigate a labyrinth of laws and regulations that can significantly influence their success. This section discusses how effective risk management in regulatory compliance impacts project managers and contributes to the overall success of fintech initiatives.

Staying Informed About Regulations

Role of Project Managers

Continuous Learning and Adaptation: The rapid evolution of blockchain technology means that regulations are constantly changing. Project managers must commit to continuous learning and staying abreast of both existing and emerging regulations. This includes attending industry conferences, participating in professional networks, and subscribing to regulatory updates.

Compliance as a Priority: Non-compliance can lead to severe legal repercussions, including fines, sanctions, and project delays. Project managers need to prioritize compliance as a core component of project planning, ensuring that all team members understand their obligations under the law. They should create systems for tracking regulatory requirements and deadlines, such as compliance calendars.

Implication for Fintech Success

Building User Trust: Compliance with regulations is essential for building and maintaining user trust. In fintech, where customers entrust their financial information to platforms, a robust compliance record assures users that their data is handled responsibly and legally.

Facilitating Smooth Project Execution: Proactive management of compliance risks can lead to smoother project execution. When project managers have a clear understanding of regulatory requirements, they can incorporate these into project timelines and deliverables, reducing the likelihood of last-minute changes or delays that could jeopardize launch dates.

Engaging with Regulators

Role of Project Managers

Establishing Communication Channels: Proactively engaging with regulatory bodies allows project managers to establish communication channels that can be invaluable for navigating the compliance landscape. This can include regular meetings with regulators, participation in public consultations, and collaboration on best practices.

Gaining Insights and Feedback: Engaging with regulators can provide project managers with insights into regulatory expectations and emerging trends. By maintaining an open dialogue, they can seek feedback on compliance strategies and adjust their approaches as necessary.

Implication for Fintech Success

Facilitating Smooth Project Launches: Building positive relationships with regulators can ease the path to project approval and facilitate smoother project launches. When regulators understand the project and its compliance measures, they are more likely to support the initiative.

Positioning for Long-Term Success: A collaborative approach with regulatory bodies can enhance a project's reputation within the fintech ecosystem. Projects that demonstrate a commitment to compliance are more likely to gain favor with regulators and stakeholders, positioning them for long-term success.

Implementing Robust Compliance Frameworks

Role of Project Managers

Coordinated Compliance Efforts: Establishing a compliance framework requires careful planning and coordination across various teams, including legal, compliance, IT, and operations. Project managers must ensure that compliance is integrated into every phase of the project lifecycle, from initial planning through to deployment and ongoing operation.

Documentation and Training: A robust compliance framework necessitates comprehensive documentation of compliance policies and procedures. Project managers are responsible for ensuring that all team members receive appropriate training on compliance matters, fostering a culture of compliance within the organization.

Implication for Fintech Success

Reducing Regulatory Risks: A strong compliance framework helps mitigate the risk of regulatory issues, which can derail projects and lead to reputational damage. By prioritizing compliance, project managers protect their projects from costly delays and potential legal ramifications.

Creating a Sustainable Business Model: Compliance is not merely about avoiding penalties; it is also about creating a sustainable business model. Projects that prioritize compliance are better positioned to adapt to regulatory changes and can more readily scale their operations in different markets.

Best Practices for Managing Regulatory Challenges

Conducting Regular Compliance Audits

Project managers should implement regular compliance audits to assess adherence to regulations and identify areas for improvement. These audits help ensure that the project remains aligned with regulatory requirements and can provide insights into evolving regulatory landscapes.

Utilizing Technology for Compliance

Leveraging technology, such as compliance management software, can streamline the monitoring and reporting of compliance activities. These tools can automate compliance checks, track regulatory changes, and facilitate documentation, allowing project managers to focus on strategic decision-making.

Establishing an Advisory Board

Creating an advisory board that includes regulatory experts and industry stakeholders can provide valuable insights into compliance challenges and best practices. This board can help project managers navigate complex regulatory landscapes and develop innovative solutions to compliance issues.

Fostering a Culture of Compliance

Project managers should cultivate a culture of compliance within the organization by emphasizing its importance at all levels. Encouraging team members to raise concerns and ask questions fosters an environment where compliance is seen as a shared responsibility rather than a burden.

Managing regulatory challenges is a crucial aspect of risk management in blockchain projects, particularly in the fintech sector. By staying informed about regulations, engaging with regulatory bodies, and implementing robust compliance frameworks, project managers can navigate the complex compliance landscape effectively. This proactive approach not only enhances project success but also builds trust among stakeholders and users, paving the way for a sustainable and reputable fintech solution.

Ensuring Data Privacy and Security in Blockchain Fintech Projects

In fintech, data privacy and security are paramount. With the growing reliance on digital platforms for financial transactions, safeguarding user information has never been more critical. Blockchain technology, while inherently secure due to its decentralized nature, still presents unique challenges and risks that project managers must address effectively. This section explores how project managers can ensure data privacy and security in blockchain fintech projects and the implications of these efforts on overall project success.

Implementing Strong Encryption Protocols

Role of Project Managers

Integration Across Development: Project managers must ensure that strong encryption measures are integrated into every phase of the development process. This includes encrypting data at rest, in transit, and during processing to protect sensitive information from unauthorized access.

Choosing the Right Algorithms: Selecting appropriate encryption algorithms is crucial. Project managers need to work closely with security experts to evaluate encryption standards, such as AES (Advanced Encryption Standard) or RSA (Rivest–Shamir–Adleman), and implement those that best fit their project requirements.

Implication for Fintech Success

Enhancing User Trust: Strong encryption serves as a critical safeguard for user data, fostering trust and confidence in the platform. In a competitive fintech market, projects that prioritize data security are more likely to attract and retain customers.

Regulatory Compliance: Encryption is often a requirement for regulatory compliance, particularly in industries dealing with sensitive financial data. By implementing robust encryption protocols, project managers ensure that their projects align with regulations such as GDPR (General Data Protection Regulation) and CCPA (California Consumer Privacy Act), reducing the risk of legal repercussions.

Adopting Decentralized Identity Solutions

Role of Project Managers

Careful Planning and Collaboration: Implementing decentralized identity solutions requires thorough planning and collaboration among stakeholders, including developers, users, and regulatory bodies. Project managers must facilitate discussions to align on goals and expectations.

User Education: Project managers need to educate users about the benefits and functionalities of decentralized identity solutions to encourage adoption and proper use.

Implication for Fintech Success

Empowering Users: Decentralized identity solutions empower users by giving them greater control over their personal information. This enhances privacy and reduces the risk of identity theft, addressing significant concerns in the fintech landscape.

Increasing User Adoption and Satisfaction: Projects that successfully implement decentralized identity frameworks can enhance user satisfaction by streamlining processes, such as onboarding and authentication, leading to higher adoption rates.

Conducting Regular Security Audits and Penetration Testing

Role of Project Managers

Establishing a Security Framework: Project managers must establish a comprehensive security framework that includes regular security audits and penetration testing as part of the project lifecycle. This involves setting clear timelines for assessments and allocating resources for conducting these evaluations.

Identifying and Addressing Vulnerabilities: Regular assessments help project managers identify vulnerabilities early and address them before they can be exploited. This proactive approach is vital for maintaining the integrity of the project.

Implication for Fintech Success

Preventing Security Breaches: Proactive security measures, such as audits and penetration testing, significantly reduce the likelihood of data breaches. A secure platform protects the project's integrity and reputation, which is crucial for long-term success in the fintech industry.

Building a Culture of Security: By prioritizing regular security evaluations, project managers cultivate a culture of security awareness within the team. This fosters accountability and encourages team members to prioritize security in their daily activities.

Educating Stakeholders on Data Privacy Best Practices

Role of Project Managers

Training Programs: Project managers should implement training programs that educate stakeholders—ranging from developers to end-users—on data privacy best practices. These programs should cover topics such as secure data handling, phishing awareness, and compliance requirements.

Creating Comprehensive Documentation: Project managers can provide comprehensive documentation outlining data privacy policies and procedures, ensuring that all stakeholders are aware of their responsibilities regarding data protection.

Implication for Fintech Success

Reducing Human Error: An informed team is less likely to make mistakes that could compromise data privacy. Training stakeholders on data privacy best practices minimizes the risk of accidental data exposure or mishandling, contributing to project stability.

Enhancing User Trust and Satisfaction: When users feel confident that their data is handled securely, their trust in the platform increases. This trust translates to greater user satisfaction and loyalty, essential factors for the success of any fintech project.

Best Practices for Ensuring Data Privacy and Security

1. Implementing Data Minimization Practices:

Adopt data minimization principles by only collecting and retaining data that is necessary for project operations. This reduces the amount of sensitive information that could be compromised in a breach.

2. Establishing Incident Response Plans:

Develop and maintain incident response plans that outline procedures for addressing data breaches and security incidents. Project managers must ensure that all team members are familiar with these plans and know their roles in case of an incident.

3. Utilizing Blockchain's Built-in Security Features:

Leverage the inherent security features of blockchain technology, such as immutability and transparency, to enhance data protection. For instance, using hash functions to verify data integrity can add an additional layer of security.

4. Regularly Updating Security Protocols:

Security threats evolve, so project managers should regularly review and update security protocols to adapt to new vulnerabilities and attack vectors. Staying informed about emerging threats is essential for maintaining robust security.

Ensuring data privacy and security in blockchain fintech projects is not just a technical necessity; it is a fundamental aspect of building trust and ensuring project success. By implementing strong encryption protocols, adopting decentralized identity solutions, conducting regular security audits, and educating stakeholders on data privacy best practices, project managers can effectively mitigate risks and enhance the credibility of their projects. In a competitive fintech landscape, prioritizing data privacy and security positions projects for long-term viability and success.

CHAPTER 5: Tools and Methodologies

The role of a project manager in blockchain-based fintech projects is both multifaceted and critical. With the rapid expansion of decentralized technologies and the increasing integration of blockchain into financial services, PMs are required to go beyond traditional project management strategies. They must not only juggle timelines, budgets, and resources but also leverage specific tools and methodologies that address the unique dynamics of blockchain technology.

This chapter serves as a comprehensive guide for project managers who are navigating the fintech space with the help of blockchain. It focuses on the core tools that enhance project oversight, as well as strategies for fostering collaboration in decentralized environments and planning resources in highly regulated and innovation-driven industries. By adopting these approaches, project managers will be better equipped to ensure the successful execution of blockchain initiatives, maintaining project integrity while aligning with fintech goals.

By examining essential project management tools, discussing the nuances of managing decentralized teams, and exploring practical resource allocation methods, this chapter offers PMs a roadmap to apply in real-world scenarios. These actionable insights will empower you to overcome the complexity of blockchain projects, ensuring that your fintech initiatives are not only efficiently run but also impactful and aligned with broader business objectives.

Essential Project Management Tools for Blockchain

Managing blockchain projects requires a transformative shift in the traditional project management mindset. While the core principles of project management—such as planning, execution, monitoring, and closing—remain foundational, project managers (PMs) must adapt their strategies to effectively handle the complexities of decentralized teams, navigate stringent compliance requirements, and respond to the rapid pace of technological advancements. This evolution involves mastering a blend of traditional project management tools alongside specialized blockchain platforms, ensuring that projects stay on course while effectively managing their inherent complexities.

Learning Blockchain-Specific Tools

In blockchain-driven fintech projects, PMs must embrace tools that address the specific technical challenges posed by decentralized systems. These tools are essential for providing critical support in areas such as security, scalability, compliance, and performance tracking. Below are several essential tools that PMs should familiarize themselves with to enhance their effectiveness in managing blockchain initiatives:

Alchemy

Alchemy stands out as a robust platform for monitoring decentralized applications (dApps) and managing blockchain infrastructure. For project managers, proficiency in Alchemy means gaining the ability to track application performance and network health in real time. This tool empowers PMs to closely oversee the development process, facilitating timely interventions when issues arise. With Alchemy, PMs can ensure that all components of the blockchain solution align with the overarching fintech objectives, ultimately driving project success. Additionally, Alchemy provides robust analytics capabilities that enable PMs to identify trends and patterns in application usage, informing strategic decisions for future iterations and enhancements.

Hyperledger

Hyperledger is pivotal for managing private blockchain networks. By mastering Hyperledger's frameworks, project managers can streamline collaboration between technical developers and various stakeholders involved in the project. This tool is particularly beneficial for navigating the complexities of regulatory compliance—an essential aspect of fintech projects. PMs can leverage Hyperledger to ensure that the blockchain solutions developed are not only secure but also adhere to industry standards and regulations, thereby reducing risks and enhancing project viability. Furthermore, Hyperledger's modular architecture allows PMs to customize their blockchain solutions according to specific organizational needs, promoting flexibility in project execution. By utilizing Hyperledger Fabric, PMs can also create permissioned networks that restrict access to sensitive data, further enhancing security and compliance.

OpenZeppelin

When overseeing the development of smart contracts, PMs must be well-versed in OpenZeppelin, which provides a comprehensive suite of security standards and best practices. By integrating OpenZeppelin into their workflow, PMs can safeguard their projects against vulnerabilities, ensuring that the smart contracts are robust and reliable. This expertise is critical in the fintech landscape, where the integrity of code directly impacts financial security and project success. Additionally, OpenZeppelin offers extensive documentation and community support, enabling PMs to stay updated on best practices and emerging security threats. By leveraging OpenZeppelin's library of reusable smart contract components, PMs can accelerate development while maintaining high-security standards.

By mastering these blockchain-specific platforms, project managers can optimize their roles in overseeing both the technical and financial dimensions of their projects, positioning themselves as invaluable assets in the blockchain fintech ecosystem. Understanding the unique capabilities of these tools enables PMs to make informed decisions that propel project outcomes and drive innovation.

Adapting Traditional Project Management Tools for Blockchain

While specialized blockchain tools are essential, traditional project management platforms remain highly valuable in the context of blockchain projects. Project managers need to adapt these familiar tools to meet the unique requirements of decentralized systems and agile development practices. Here are several traditional tools that can be effectively employed in this context:

Jira

Jira is renowned for its robust capabilities in managing agile workflows, making it particularly suited for the iterative nature of blockchain development. By leveraging Jira to set up backlogs and sprints, project managers can create a structured environment that encourages teams to work collaboratively and transparently. This setup aids in managing and reviewing progress while allowing PMs to maintain a pulse on project timelines, ensuring that critical milestones are met. Jira's integration with development tools such as GitHub and Bitbucket facilitates seamless communication among team members, enhancing project visibility. Furthermore, Jira's reporting features allow PMs to generate insights into team performance and project health, enabling data-driven adjustments to workflows as needed.

Asana

Asana is a powerful task management tool that enables project managers to break down complex blockchain projects into manageable tasks. This feature enhances transparency across various teams, which is vital in fintech initiatives requiring coordination between developers, compliance officers, and financial analysts. Asana's user-friendly interface allows PMs to track contributions from each department easily, facilitating better communication and collaboration throughout the project lifecycle. Additionally, Asana's timeline and calendar views provide visual aids for project planning, helping teams stay aligned on deadlines and responsibilities. By utilizing Asana's automation capabilities, PMs can streamline task assignments and notifications, reducing manual effort and ensuring that team members remain engaged.

Monday.com

For project managers seeking a visual representation of their project's progress, Monday.com offers customizable dashboards that simplify tracking resource allocation, project timelines, and interdependencies. PMs can utilize this tool to keep team members aligned and address any potential issues promptly. By having a clear visual layout of the project's status, project managers can make informed decisions and avert costly delays before they escalate. Monday.com's integration with various applications allows for a holistic view of project progress, combining data from different sources into one platform. Moreover, its automation features enable PMs to set reminders and recurring tasks, enhancing productivity and ensuring that important milestones are consistently met.

When tailored to meet the needs of blockchain projects, these traditional tools provide PMs with the visibility and control necessary to guide their teams toward successful project outcomes in the fintech arena. By embracing both specialized blockchain tools and traditional project management platforms, PMs can enhance their effectiveness and drive their projects to success in this dynamic and rapidly evolving industry. This dual approach not only equips PMs to manage projects more effectively but also fosters a culture of collaboration and innovation within their teams.

By investing time in understanding and mastering these essential project management tools—both specialized and traditional—project managers can significantly enhance their effectiveness in the blockchain fintech space. The ability to adapt and apply a diverse toolkit tailored to the unique challenges of blockchain projects will position PMs as key drivers of innovation and success within their organizations. As blockchain continues to reshape the fintech landscape, the role of PMs will be increasingly vital in ensuring that projects are executed efficiently, comply with regulations, and deliver value to stakeholders.

Collaboration and Communication in Decentralized Teams

Managing decentralized teams presents unique challenges in communication and collaboration, especially in the blockchain fintech sector where time zones, cultural differences, regulatory considerations, and highly specialized technical knowledge all come into play. To effectively manage these teams, project managers (PMs) must leverage tools that not only keep communication flowing but also foster a collaborative environment that drives productivity, innovation, and adherence to project timelines.

Decentralized teams—comprising developers, compliance officers, financial experts, and more—can span across geographies, often with little to no physical interaction. The need for reliable, real-time communication tools becomes essential to avoid misunderstandings, delays, and misalignment with project objectives. Below are several critical tools and platforms designed to enhance communication for blockchain teams, each offering unique features that cater to the decentralized nature of these teams.

Communication Tools for Blockchain Teams

Slack

Slack has established itself as the go-to tool for decentralized team communication, offering a balance between structure and flexibility. Its project-specific channels and advanced integration features make it ideal for blockchain teams, where multiple discussions—technical, strategic, compliance-related

—need to happen simultaneously, but in an organized and accessible way.

Project-Specific Channels: One of the key features that make Slack effective for decentralized teams is its ability to create distinct channels for different projects, teams, or topics. This allows project managers to maintain focused, structured conversations, avoiding confusion and ensuring that important discussions aren't lost in the noise. For example, a PM could create separate channels for smart contract development, regulatory compliance, marketing strategy, and financial audits, all within the same overarching project workspace.

Integration with Other Tools: Slack's extensive library of integrations with platforms like Jira, GitHub, and Trello means that task management, code reviews, and issue tracking can be handled without leaving the chat environment. This is especially useful for blockchain teams where rapid development, testing, and deployment cycles are common. Integrating Jira, for example, allows developers to receive real-time updates on bug fixes or sprint changes directly in Slack, keeping everyone informed and aligned.

Slackbot and Automation: Automating routine tasks through Slackbot can save significant time for PMs. For instance, setting automated reminders for deadlines, task completions, or sprint reviews ensures that no one misses critical dates, even when team members are spread across different time zones. Similarly, Slackbot can be configured to summarize key discussion points from meetings, keeping everyone on the same page.

Microsoft Teams

For blockchain teams that deal with sensitive fintech data, security is paramount. Microsoft Teams offers a robust alternative to Slack, with a strong emphasis on data protection, seamless integration with Office 365, and the ability to host meetings and manage tasks in a secure, compliant environment.

Secure Document Sharing and Communication: In blockchain fintech, where intellectual property, financial transactions, and client data need to be handled with utmost security, Microsoft Teams shines. With its end-to-end encryption and compliance with international data regulations like GDPR and HIPAA, PMs can be assured that sensitive documents and communications are protected. This is particularly crucial when sharing compliance reports, financial forecasts, or smart contract code between departments.

Cross-Departmental Collaboration: PMs can use Teams to bridge gaps between decentralized teams and other departments—such as compliance, legal, or marketing—by creating dedicated workspaces for collaborative projects. For example, in a fintech project developing a new decentralized lending platform, the legal team might work closely with the developers to ensure that the product adheres to relevant regulations. Microsoft Teams allows them to collaborate in real-time while sharing sensitive documents securely.

Integration with Office 365: Teams integrates seamlessly with other Microsoft Office applications like Word, Excel, and PowerPoint. This enables decentralized teams to co-author documents, create project reports, or review financial models in real time, ensuring that the most up-to-date versions are available to everyone. PMs can also leverage Microsoft Planner (integrated within Teams) to create tasks, assign them to team members, and track progress within the same environment, thus simplifying task management and communication.

Discord

Discord was originally designed for gaming communities, it has rapidly become a favorite tool among blockchain development communities due to its flexibility in facilitating both formal and informal communication. Discord offers a blend of structured project discussion and casual collaboration, fostering a more open and transparent team environment.

Community Building and Collaboration: One of the unique features of Discord is its ability to host large, active communities around specific topics or projects. PMs can create dedicated servers with multiple channels—each focused on different aspects of the project. For instance, in a blockchain project that involves multiple partnerships (e.g., third-party dApp developers, compliance teams, and marketing agencies), each partner could have its own dedicated channel within the Discord server, facilitating collaboration while keeping conversations structured.

Voice and Video Channels: Discord's voice and video communication features are highly effective for quick team meetings, brainstorming sessions, and technical discussions. Unlike traditional conference calls, Discord's real-time voice channels allow teams to jump in and out of meetings as needed, fostering a more spontaneous and collaborative atmosphere. This can be especially beneficial for decentralized blockchain teams that may need to troubleshoot a technical issue on the fly.

Custom Bots and Automation: Like Slack, Discord supports the use of custom bots to automate routine tasks such as sending project updates, summarizing meeting notes, or notifying teams of new code commits. Bots can also track user activity or assign roles automatically based on user actions, making team management more efficient.

Implementing Methodologies for Managing Remote Teams

In addition to effective communication tools, managing remote blockchain teams requires adopting project management methodologies that support decentralized, agile work environments. The methodologies discussed below allow PMs to maintain flexibility, accountability, and adaptability across distributed teams.

Agile

Agile methodologies have long been championed in the tech industry for their ability to break large projects into manageable, iterative cycles. In blockchain fintech, where innovation happens rapidly, and regulatory requirements may change overnight, Agile methodologies offer a framework that allows decentralized teams to remain nimble and responsive.

Sprint-Based Development: Blockchain development often involves a high degree of uncertainty, where technical challenges and new opportunities can arise unexpectedly. By dividing the project into short, iterative sprints, PMs can keep the team focused on delivering incremental improvements while retaining the flexibility to pivot or adjust based on feedback or new requirements.

Collaboration Across Time Zones: Agile's emphasis on daily standups and frequent feedback loops allows decentralized teams working across different time zones to stay aligned. PMs can schedule asynchronous check-ins, where team members update their progress and identify roadblocks in a shared document or Slack channel, allowing others to review updates at their convenience.

Cross-Functional Teams: Blockchain projects typically involve collaboration between various functional groups—developers, financial experts, compliance officers, and legal teams. Agile promotes the integration of cross-functional teams, encouraging knowledge sharing and faster decision-making. For instance, in a project that aims to integrate blockchain into payment systems, developers might work directly with compliance officers to ensure that the new system adheres to financial regulations.

Scrum

Scrum, a specific Agile framework, is particularly effective for managing blockchain projects that require frequent feedback and incremental progress toward a larger goal. Scrum's focus on iterative work processes, role definition, and frequent reviews ensures that project goals are consistently met while maintaining high levels of flexibility.

Defined Roles and Clear Responsibilities: Scrum introduces defined roles such as the Scrum Master, Product Owner, and Development Team, ensuring that all team members have clear responsibilities. This clarity is especially important in decentralized teams where communication gaps can lead to misunderstandings. The Scrum Master, for example, acts as a facilitator, ensuring that remote teams have the tools and resources they need to stay productive and aligned with project objectives.

Daily Standups and Sprint Reviews: Daily standups provide team members the opportunity to share their progress, identify roadblocks, and recalibrate priorities. This transparency is vital in blockchain fintech projects, where regulatory or market changes may require teams to adjust their approach quickly. Sprint reviews at the end of each iteration allow PMs and stakeholders to assess progress, provide feedback, and ensure that the project remains on track.

Backlog Refinement: Scrum allows PMs to maintain a prioritized backlog of tasks and features, enabling decentralized teams to stay focused on the most critical aspects of the project. This prioritization is crucial in fintech, where market demands and compliance requirements may shift suddenly.

DevOps

The DevOps approach, which combines development and operations practices, is particularly well-suited for blockchain fintech projects. Given the continuous development, testing, and deployment cycles required in decentralized applications (dApps), DevOps ensures that teams can deliver high-quality software efficiently and securely.

Continuous Integration and Continuous Deployment (CI/CD): DevOps emphasizes the automation of testing and deployment processes, allowing blockchain applications to be developed, tested, and deployed continuously. This automation reduces the risk of errors and accelerates the delivery of new features, ensuring that blockchain fintech products remain competitive in the market.

Cross-Functional Collaboration: In the DevOps model, developers and operations teams work closely together, ensuring that new features or updates are not only developed quickly but also deployed and maintained efficiently. In a blockchain fintech project, this collaboration can help address the unique challenges of decentralized systems—such as scalability and network stability—more effectively.

Real-Time Monitoring and Feedback: Continuous monitoring of deployed applications allows PMs to gather real-time feedback and quickly address issues as they arise. In the fintech space, where security breaches or transaction delays can have severe consequences, DevOps practices help ensure that blockchain applications remain stable, secure, and compliant.

Successfully managing decentralized blockchain teams requires a combination of effective communication tools and flexible project management methodologies. Tools like Slack, Microsoft Teams, and Discord provide decentralized teams with the means to collaborate efficiently, while Agile, Scrum, and DevOps methodologies ensure that teams remain adaptable, accountable, and aligned with project objectives. By adopting these best practices, project managers can overcome the unique challenges of decentralized work and drive the success of blockchain fintech initiatives.

Resource Planning and Allocation

In blockchain fintech projects, success is intricately tied to how well project managers (PMs) allocate resources—whether it's skilled personnel, technology infrastructure, or financial capital. Unlike conventional projects, blockchain fintech initiatives involve a combination of emerging technologies, regulatory challenges, and highly specialized talent. This makes resource planning and allocation both complex and critical. In this section, we'll explore not only the tools that support effective resource management but also the broader strategies PMs should adopt to navigate the unique demands of blockchain in fintech.

At the depth of blockchain fintech project management lies the delicate balance between technical execution and regulatory compliance. It's easy to get caught up in the technical complexities of blockchain, but PMs must always keep an eye on the bigger picture—ensuring resources are used efficiently and aligned with both project goals and compliance requirements. Misallocation of resources, whether it's underestimating financial needs or improperly distributing skilled talent, can lead to costly delays or even project failure.

Mastering Resource Management Tools and Strategies

Managing resources in blockchain fintech goes far beyond simply scheduling tasks or tracking timelines. PMs must make decisions based on real-time data, team capacity, regulatory considerations, and the unique challenges that arise from working with decentralized technologies. This requires a combination of advanced tools and strategic foresight. Below, we examine key tools and how PMs can integrate them into a broader resource management strategy.

Mavenlink: Predictive Resource Allocation for Blockchain Projects

Mavenlink is a powerful tool for PMs looking to enhance their resource planning capabilities through predictive analytics. In blockchain fintech, where project scopes can evolve rapidly, having predictive insight into future resource needs is crucial. Mavenlink's detailed analytics allow PMs to anticipate how staffing requirements may change as the project progresses through various phases, such as research, development, testing, and deployment.

Real-Time Resource Forecasting: PMs can use Mavenlink's resource forecasting capabilities to predict when specific skill sets (e.g., blockchain developers, cryptography experts, financial analysts) will be needed, preventing bottlenecks caused by resource shortages.

Preventing Project Overload: Fintech projects often require compliance with stringent regulations, adding layers of complexity that strain resources. Mavenlink helps PMs balance technical needs with compliance efforts, ensuring that teams are neither under-resourced nor overburdened.

By integrating Mavenlink into their project management strategy, PMs can preemptively address staffing challenges, forecast budgetary needs, and adjust timelines to maintain project momentum without compromising quality.

Float: Adapting to Dynamic Resource Needs in Blockchain Projects

Blockchain projects, especially in fintech, are inherently dynamic. The pace of technological change and the iterative nature of blockchain development often result in shifting priorities. Float is a resource management tool that allows PMs to track team availability and adjust allocations in real time, making it easier to respond to these shifts without causing major project disruptions.

Real-Time Capacity Tracking: With decentralized teams, which are common in blockchain projects, keeping track of team members' availability and workloads becomes challenging. Float allows PMs to monitor team capacity in real time, preventing overcommitment and ensuring that no team is stretched too thin.

Dynamic Task Allocation: The ability to dynamically adjust task allocations is vital in blockchain projects, where a sudden regulatory update or technical hurdle may require reallocating resources on the fly. Float's flexible task management capabilities give PMs the agility to respond quickly to unexpected changes.

The use of Float enhances PMs' ability to ensure that the right people are working on the right tasks at the right time, optimizing productivity and maintaining project timelines despite the complexities of blockchain fintech environments.

Wrike: Ensuring Comprehensive Project Visibility

In blockchain fintech, projects often involve multiple teams working on different aspects of the project simultaneously. Wrike offers PMs comprehensive project visibility, allowing them to track resources across these teams, monitor progress, and adjust allocations when necessary.

Visual Resource Dashboards: Wrike's customizable dashboards provide PMs with a visual overview of resource usage across all phases of the project. For blockchain fintech, this is particularly useful when coordinating between technical teams, legal compliance teams, and financial auditors.

Automated Reporting: Wrike's automated reporting capabilities allow PMs to generate real-time updates on resource allocation, making it easier to keep stakeholders informed. In blockchain fintech projects, where transparency and stakeholder engagement are critical, Wrike ensures that PMs can provide detailed resource reports on demand.

Using Wrike in tandem with other resource management tools allows PMs to maintain a high level of control over resource distribution, ensuring that blockchain projects proceed smoothly, with full visibility into each aspect of the resource allocation process.

Budgeting and Cost Allocation in Blockchain Projects

Budget management is a key aspect of resource planning, and in the blockchain fintech space, it presents unique challenges. The high costs associated with blockchain development, coupled with regulatory compliance expenses, make budgeting a crucial factor in project success. Effective budgeting ensures that projects remain financially viable while meeting technical and regulatory demands. PMs must develop strong budgeting skills and leverage advanced financial management tools to track expenses, forecast financial needs, and optimize cost allocation.

Oracle NetSuite: Comprehensive Financial Management

Oracle NetSuite is a comprehensive cloud-based tool that

allows PMs to manage all aspects of a project's financial health. In blockchain fintech, where financial transparency and regulatory compliance are paramount, NetSuite provides the tools necessary to keep track of every dollar spent, ensuring that the project stays within budget.

Expense Tracking and Budget Control: With Oracle NetSuite, PMs can monitor project expenses in real time, track vendor costs, and ensure that budget allocations are used efficiently. For blockchain projects, where unexpected costs can arise from technical challenges or regulatory changes, having detailed expense tracking is crucial.

Financial Forecasting and Scenario Planning: NetSuite's forecasting tools allow PMs to create financial models that predict future expenses based on current spending trends. This helps PMs anticipate when additional funding may be required, avoiding the financial pitfalls that can derail a blockchain project.

Primavera P6: Advanced Budgeting for Large-Scale Blockchain Projects

For PMs overseeing large-scale blockchain fintech projects, Primavera P6 offers advanced budgeting and cost management features. Primavera is designed for complex projects that involve multiple stakeholders, making it ideal for blockchain initiatives that require detailed financial oversight and long-term planning.

Detailed Cost Breakdown: Primavera P6 allows PMs to create detailed cost breakdowns, tracking expenses for every phase of the project, from development to deployment. This level of granularity is essential in fintech, where costs must be allocated not only to development but also to compliance, auditing, and security.

Stakeholder Communication: One of the key challenges in blockchain projects is keeping stakeholders informed about the project's financial health. Primavera P6 provides PMs with the ability to generate detailed financial reports that offer stakeholders a clear view of how funds are being used and whether the project is staying within budget.

By mastering financial tools like Oracle NetSuite and Primavera P6, PMs can ensure that their blockchain fintech projects are both financially sustainable and compliant with industry regulations. Effective cost management reduces the risk of project delays caused by financial shortfalls, helping PMs deliver successful outcomes on time and within budget.

Strategic Resource Allocation: "Going Beyond the Tools"

While tools play a critical role in resource planning and allocation, successful project management in blockchain fintech also requires adopting broader strategies that align resources with project goals. PMs should not view resource allocation as a static process; it must be dynamic and flexible, constantly evolving to meet the changing demands of the project. Here are some key strategies PMs can employ:

Prioritize Regulatory Compliance: In fintech, compliance is non-negotiable. PMs must allocate sufficient resources—both financial and human—to ensure that compliance requirements are met at every stage of the project. This may involve hiring legal experts, conducting regular audits, or investing in compliance management tools.

Balance Technical and Financial Resources: Blockchain projects often require substantial investment in both technology and personnel. PMs must strike a balance between allocating resources to technical development (such as hiring blockchain developers or investing in new technologies) and financial management (such as budgeting for regulatory compliance and auditing).

Optimize Talent Utilization: Skilled professionals are often the most valuable resource in a blockchain fintech project. PMs must ensure that key team members are not overburdened and that their expertise is applied to the most critical tasks. This may involve redistributing workloads or bringing in additional talent to fill gaps.

By combining the right tools with strategic resource allocation, PMs can navigate the complexities of blockchain fintech projects, ensuring that resources are used efficiently, budgets are maintained, and projects are delivered successfully.

CHAPTER 6: Case Studies of Successful Blockchain Projects

As we approach the culmination of our study into blockchain's role in fintech, it becomes imperative to examine tangible examples of success. Real-world case studies provide invaluable insights into how blockchain technology can streamline processes, enhance transparency, and foster innovation in the financial services sector. More importantly, these examples illustrate the pivotal role project managers play in navigating the complexities of blockchain implementation.

In this chapter, we will analyze successful fintech projects that have harnessed the power of blockchain. We will focus on the implications for project management and the strategies employed to achieve success. By learning from these case studies, project managers can glean best practices to replicate similar outcomes in their organizations.

Analyzing Successful Fintech Projects Utilizing Blockchain

For project managers, blockchain's application in fintech projects presents both opportunities and complexities that require a nuanced understanding of the technology. As we drift into real-world examples, it becomes clear that successful blockchain implementation hinges on well-orchestrated project management practices.

The following case studies illustrate the diverse ways blockchain has been utilized in financial services, highlighting key project management strategies that contributed to each project's success. These lessons are critical for project managers overseeing blockchain adoption in fintech, as they offer practical guidance on managing stakeholders, mitigating risks, and driving innovation.

1. Ripple (XRP) — "Revolutionizing Cross-Border Payments"

Ripple has redefined how cross-border payments are processed, disrupting traditional banking models that rely on a series of intermediaries to transfer funds internationally. Ripple's **distributed ledger technology (DLT)** allows transactions to occur within seconds, offering a low-cost and efficient alternative to existing financial infrastructure.

Key Project Management Insights:

Stakeholder Engagement: Ripple's widespread adoption among financial institutions stems from its ability to foster strong relationships with banks, payment providers, and regulatory bodies. Project managers must place a heavy emphasis on stakeholder engagement by creating clear communication channels and ensuring that all parties have a shared understanding of the project's value. Ripple's continuous collaboration with global institutions ensured it remained agile and responsive to the needs of its partners.

Practical Tip: Establish a formal communication plan at the onset of blockchain projects to provide regular updates, gather feedback, and make necessary adjustments based on stakeholder needs. Stakeholders in fintech often have varying expectations, so clear, continuous dialogue can prevent misalignment.

Agile Methodologies: Ripple employed agile project management, which allowed the team to break down complex goals into smaller, manageable iterations. This iterative approach enabled Ripple to rapidly evolve its product to meet market demands, staying competitive in the fast-moving fintech industry. For project managers, agile methodologies foster flexibility, allowing teams to adapt to regulatory changes or shifts in the financial ecosystem.

Practical Tip: Implement short sprints and regular retrospectives in blockchain projects. This iterative model allows teams to respond quickly to external shifts, such as regulatory developments or emerging customer needs.

Risk Management: Early in its development, Ripple identified potential regulatory and legal risks, particularly around the use of cryptocurrency in traditional banking systems. Project managers played a crucial role in mitigating these risks by collaborating with legal teams and crafting strategies that ensured compliance across different jurisdictions. This preemptive focus on compliance was key to Ripple's success.

Practical Tip: Conduct a comprehensive risk assessment at the beginning of the project. This should include potential legal, regulatory, and operational risks, along with mitigation strategies to ensure that the project remains compliant and on track.

2. Chainalysis - "Enhancing Blockchain Compliance

and Transparency"

Chainalysis offers blockchain analysis tools that provide critical insights into cryptocurrency transactions, helping financial institutions maintain regulatory compliance. As the fintech world grapples with increasing scrutiny over cryptocurrency use, Chainalysis has positioned itself as a vital solution for tracing illicit activities and providing transparency in blockchain transactions.

Key Project Management Insights:

Data-Driven Decision Making: Chainalysis's approach relies heavily on the analysis of vast amounts of blockchain data, enabling financial institutions to make informed decisions about compliance and risk. Project managers in blockchain projects can harness data as a core part of their decision-making processes, ensuring that project goals are supported by actionable insights.

> *Practical Tip:* Incorporate data analytics into your project's key performance indicators (KPIs). This allows teams to monitor project progress and adapt strategies in real time based on data-driven insights.

Adaptability to Regulations: The regulatory environment surrounding cryptocurrencies is highly dynamic. Chainalysis had to remain adaptable, regularly updating its platform to meet new compliance standards. Project managers should expect regulatory changes throughout the life cycle of a blockchain project and ensure that their teams are prepared to adapt quickly.

Practical Tip: Establish a dedicated regulatory task force within your project team. This group should monitor regulatory trends, provide regular updates, and work closely with developers to ensure compliance without compromising innovation.

Team Collaboration and Cross-Functional Coordination: Chainalysis's success also comes from its effective coordination between technical teams, compliance experts, and project managers. Ensuring cross-functional collaboration allowed the project to stay compliant while also driving innovation. This highlights the need for a collaborative culture in blockchain projects.

Practical Tip: Implement regular cross-functional meetings that involve legal, technical, and project management teams. These meetings can help identify compliance issues early and allow for collaborative problem-solving.

3. Uniswap — "The Rise of Decentralized Finance (DeFi)"

Uniswap is one of the leading decentralized finance (DeFi) protocols, enabling peer-to-peer trading of cryptocurrencies without intermediaries. Built on Ethereum, Uniswap utilizes smart contracts to facilitate trades directly between users. This marks a fundamental shift towards decentralization in finance, empowering users while reducing reliance on centralized exchanges.

Key Project Management Insights:

Innovation Management: One of the most striking aspects

of Uniswap's development was its innovative liquidity model. The protocol introduced an automated market-making (AMM) system, which eliminated the need for order books. For project managers, embracing innovation is critical, especially when implementing cutting-edge technologies like blockchain. This requires fostering a culture that encourages experimentation and iterative improvements.

Practical Tip: In blockchain projects, innovation should be treated as a core objective. Set up a framework that allows your team to test new features on a small scale before rolling them out more widely.

Community Engagement: DeFi projects, by their nature, rely heavily on community involvement. Uniswap's success can be largely attributed to its strong community of developers, users, and token holders. For project managers, building and maintaining a vibrant community is crucial for blockchain projects, particularly in decentralized ecosystems. Engaging with users through feedback loops and governance systems can help drive adoption and innovation.

Practical Tip: Establish a user feedback system where community members can provide input on project development. Open channels of communication foster loyalty and offer valuable insights that can be integrated into future project iterations.

Scalability Considerations: Like many Ethereum-based projects, Uniswap faced scalability challenges as user demand increased. Managing growth without compromising performance is a key challenge for project managers. Uniswap's ability to scale successfully relied on project managers anticipating future growth and planning for infrastructure upgrades in advance.

> ***Practical Tip:*** Scalability should be a priority from the outset of a blockchain project. Project managers need to ensure that the technical infrastructure is capable of supporting future demand and that contingency plans are in place for scaling without disrupting user experience.

These case studies highlight the diverse ways blockchain can transform the financial services sector. Ripple's innovation in cross-border payments, Chainalysis's focus on compliance, and Uniswap's decentralized trading model demonstrate the breadth of blockchain's potential in fintech.

For project managers, the common thread across these projects is the emphasis on adaptability, collaboration, and risk management. By fostering strong stakeholder relationships, employing agile methodologies, leveraging data-driven insights, and planning for growth, project managers can navigate the unique challenges of blockchain implementation and lead their teams to success.

Lessons Learned from Real-World Projects

Drawing from the previous case studies, several crucial lessons emerge for project managers seeking to successfully implement blockchain solutions within fintech. These lessons provide a framework for managing the inherent complexities of blockchain while capitalizing on its transformative potential. Each lesson is designed to equip project managers with the practical tools and strategies needed to deliver results in a rapidly evolving technological landscape.

1. Effective Stakeholder Engagement

One of the most critical factors in the success of blockchain projects is **proactive stakeholder engagement**. Blockchain projects often involve a complex network of participants, including financial institutions, regulators, developers, customers, and, in some cases, a decentralized community. Ensuring that each of these stakeholders is aligned with the project's objectives is paramount.

Early Involvement: Projects like Ripple and Chainalysis succeeded because they engaged key stakeholders from the start, ensuring that their needs were considered at every stage of the project. This early buy-in allowed project managers to gather valuable feedback, anticipate potential objections, and make course corrections early in the process.

Practical Tip: Organize stakeholder workshops early in the project to define roles, responsibilities, and expectations. Make it a continuous process to update stakeholders on project progress and challenges through formal reports, presentations, and face-to-face or virtual meetings.

Trust and Transparency: Blockchain inherently promotes transparency, but that transparency needs to be mirrored in stakeholder communications. The more open and transparent a project is with its stakeholders, the more likely it is to earn their trust, which is critical for adoption, especially in the financial sector where trust is foundational.

Practical Tip: Use a transparent communication platform that allows stakeholders to track the project's progress in real-time. This could be a project management tool that provides dashboards showing key milestones, deliverables, and challenges.

Stakeholder Feedback Loops: Successful projects ensure a two-way communication channel between stakeholders and project managers. Continuously gathering feedback allows the project to adapt to evolving needs, especially when working with external partners or regulatory bodies.

Practical Tip: Establish feedback loops that regularly solicit input from stakeholders, particularly on compliance and risk factors. Quarterly reviews with key stakeholders can help recalibrate project goals in alignment with external conditions like regulatory shifts.

2. Agility and Adaptability

Blockchain technology is evolving at a rapid pace, and the regulatory frameworks that govern its use are far from static. This means project managers must adopt **agile practices** that allow for flexibility and quick pivots in response to new developments.

Iterative Development: Fintech companies like Ripple and Uniswap leveraged agile methodologies to continuously improve their solutions. By breaking down complex projects into smaller, manageable sprints, they could focus on achieving incremental goals while maintaining the flexibility to shift strategies when necessary.

Practical Tip: Implement agile frameworks such as Scrum or Kanban for blockchain projects. Use short development cycles (e.g., two-week sprints) to test and iterate on features while remaining responsive to regulatory changes or technological advancements.

Regulatory Adaptability: As illustrated by Chainalysis, the regulatory landscape in fintech is one of the most fluid elements of blockchain implementation. Project managers must build flexibility into their project plans to accommodate evolving legal frameworks without delaying the project timeline or compromising its objectives.

Practical Tip: Create a regulatory task force within your team that tracks legal updates and provides regular briefings. This ensures that the project remains adaptable and compliant, even in the face of new regulations.

Embrace Change: Agility isn't just about software development —it's a mindset. Project managers should foster a culture that encourages experimentation and adaptability. Fintech projects that successfully embrace change can navigate disruptions and capitalize on emerging opportunities.

Practical Tip: Regularly revisit project goals and timelines to ensure they remain aligned with current realities. Conduct bi-monthly retrospectives with your team to reflect on what worked, what didn't, and what needs to change in the next iteration.

3. Strategic Risk Management

Blockchain implementation in fintech faces unique regulatory, operational, and technological risks. Projects that thrive in this environment do so by embedding **risk management strategies** into every phase of their operations.

Regulatory Risk: The most immediate challenge for fintech projects using blockchain is navigating the regulatory maze.

Ripple's ability to identify and address potential regulatory barriers early in the project lifecycle was key to its success. Proactive risk management, including ongoing legal consultations and compliance audits, is essential.

Practical Tip: Develop a risk management plan that identifies regulatory, operational, and market risks. Assign risk owners who are responsible for monitoring and mitigating risks related to their areas of expertise, and establish contingency plans for each identified risk.

Operational Risk: Managing the operational risks associated with blockchain, such as system downtime or smart contract vulnerabilities, requires careful planning. Uniswap's challenges with scalability highlight the importance of operational preparedness in blockchain projects.

Practical Tip: Build resilience into your project by conducting regular risk assessments, incorporating security testing for smart contracts, and planning for infrastructure scalability as user demand increases.

Financial and Reputational Risk: The financial industry is highly sensitive to disruptions, and blockchain projects must carefully manage their public image, particularly when dealing with customer funds. Chainalysis, for instance, emphasized transparency and compliance to build trust with institutions and mitigate reputational risks.

Practical Tip: Implement comprehensive communication strategies that anticipate potential risks and have prepared messaging in place. This is particularly important when launching a product or feature to ensure public perception is managed effectively.

4. Data-Driven Project Management

One of blockchain's most significant advantages is its ability to generate **real-time data** that can be used to inform project decisions. Project managers who leverage this data can improve transparency, accountability, and resource allocation throughout the lifecycle of the project.

Real-Time Monitoring: Blockchain provides an unprecedented level of transparency, enabling project managers to track transactions, contracts, and progress in real time. This capability is crucial for adjusting timelines, reallocating resources, or mitigating risks as soon as they arise.

Practical Tip: Implement blockchain analytics tools that provide real-time updates on the project's status. Use these tools to track KPIs such as transaction volumes, processing times, and network efficiency, allowing for rapid course corrections when necessary.

Informed Decision-Making: Chainalysis demonstrated the value of data in compliance and risk management. Project managers should integrate data-driven decision-making into all phases of the project, from initial planning to execution and post-implementation evaluation.

Practical Tip: Incorporate data analytics into your project dashboard to visualize key performance metrics. Create automated reports that are shared with stakeholders to keep everyone informed on project progress and outcomes.

Resource Optimization: Data-driven insights can also help project managers allocate resources more efficiently. By analyzing blockchain data, project managers can determine where bottlenecks occur and allocate additional resources to address those challenges.

> ***Practical Tip:*** Use predictive analytics to forecast resource needs based on data trends. For example, if transaction volumes spike during certain periods, additional resources may be allocated in advance to accommodate increased demand.

The lessons derived from real-world blockchain projects provide a comprehensive roadmap for project managers in fintech. Effective stakeholder engagement, agility in project execution, proactive risk management, and data-driven decision-making are all essential components of a successful blockchain project. By applying these lessons, project managers can not only navigate the complexities of blockchain implementation but also position their projects for long-term success in the competitive fintech space.

Best Practices and Strategies to Replicate Success

Replicating the success of pioneering blockchain projects requires a careful balance of strategic foresight, robust project management, and an adaptable mindset. The complexity of fintech, combined with the rapidly evolving blockchain space, demands that project managers adopt best practices tailored to the unique challenges presented by this innovative technology. By adhering to the following strategies, project managers can maximize the chances of success while mitigating risks and driving long-term value for their organizations.

1. Prioritize Stakeholder Collaboration

One of the most vital lessons from successful blockchain projects is the importance of **early and continuous stakeholder collaboration**. Given the complexity and novelty of blockchain technology, gaining stakeholder buy-in from the outset ensures that everyone—from the development team to external partners—remains aligned with the project's objectives.

Transparent Communication Channels: Clear, open communication fosters trust and ensures that all stakeholders, including regulators, customers, and internal teams, understand the project's goals, progress, and challenges. Project managers should establish transparent communication channels that allow for real-time updates and feedback loops.

Practical Tip: Set up a shared communication platform (e.g., Slack, Microsoft Teams, or a project management tool) that all stakeholders can access. This platform should provide real-time insights into project milestones, potential roadblocks, and status updates. Regular meetings and reporting cycles (such as weekly stand-ups or monthly progress reports) should be incorporated into the project schedule.

Cross-Functional Teams: Successful blockchain projects often involve diverse teams, including software developers, legal experts, finance professionals, and user experience (UX) designers. Bringing these stakeholders into the fold early helps create a holistic approach to project management.

Practical Tip: Form cross-functional teams during the planning phase. Assign roles and responsibilities clearly, and ensure that every team member understands the project's broader business and technical objectives. Use collaboration tools like Trello or Asana to track progress and delegate tasks efficiently.

Building Trust with External Stakeholders: Blockchain's decentralized nature means many projects rely on external stakeholders, such as financial institutions, users, and regulators. Building and maintaining trust with these groups is crucial, particularly in fintech where regulatory compliance and security are paramount.

Practical Tip: For external stakeholder engagement, create customized presentations or demos that showcase how the blockchain project aligns with their specific needs. Demonstrating how the solution enhances security, reduces costs, or improves efficiency can significantly enhance stakeholder confidence.

2. Develop Robust Risk Management Plans

Successful blockchain projects proactively anticipate risks, both technical and regulatory, and put measures in place to mitigate those risks before they threaten the project's success. In the fintech space, **strategic risk management** is essential to navigate the uncertainties surrounding blockchain adoption, scalability, and security.

Comprehensive Risk Assessment: Blockchain introduces new risks, particularly around scalability, security, and regulatory compliance. Project managers must conduct thorough risk assessments at the start of the project and continue to reassess as the project evolves. Potential risks should be identified, categorized, and addressed before they escalate.

Practical Tip: Use a structured risk assessment framework, such as SWOT (Strengths, Weaknesses, Opportunities, Threats) analysis, to identify risks in areas like security vulnerabilities, regulatory uncertainty, and market volatility. Update the risk matrix regularly, with specific contingency plans for each identified risk.

Regulatory Risk Management: Projects such as Chainalysis underscore the importance of staying ahead of regulatory changes. Given the sensitive nature of financial data, fintech blockchain projects need to be particularly vigilant about compliance.

Practical Tip: Engage a dedicated legal or compliance officer within the project team. Regularly consult with regulatory bodies and legal experts to ensure that the project adheres to the latest standards and is prepared for any sudden regulatory changes.

Security and Operational Risk: Blockchain's decentralized architecture reduces some risks but introduces new ones, especially around cybersecurity and scalability. Project managers must ensure that the project includes robust security protocols, such as encryption, multi-signature wallets, and regular audits.

Practical Tip: Conduct periodic security audits and implement continuous penetration testing throughout the project lifecycle. Assign security leads within the project team to focus on identifying and resolving potential vulnerabilities.

3. Leverage Community Input (for DeFi and

Decentralized Projects)

In the decentralized finance (DeFi) sector, the community is often integral to the success and growth of a project. **Fostering a strong community** not only builds trust and credibility but also encourages innovation by leveraging the diverse input of users, developers, and stakeholders.

Community Engagement for Innovation: Projects like Uniswap have demonstrated that community involvement can lead to groundbreaking innovations, such as the liquidity pools model that revolutionized decentralized trading. Project managers in DeFi should actively involve their user base in decision-making processes and product development.

> *Practical Tip:* Establish a governance model that allows community members to vote on key decisions, such as protocol upgrades or fee structures. Platforms like DAOstack or Snapshot provide decentralized governance solutions for community input.

Incentivizing Participation: Engaging the community often requires incentivization, particularly in decentralized projects. Offering rewards or tokens for participation can increase engagement and foster a sense of ownership among users.

> *Practical Tip:* Create incentive programs for your community, such as reward-based campaigns for developers who contribute code or users who provide valuable feedback. Use bounty programs to encourage testing and auditing of smart contracts.

4. Plan for Scalability

As blockchain solutions become more widely adopted, **scalability** becomes a significant concern. Projects that fail to anticipate future growth may face performance degradation, which can lead to user dissatisfaction, higher costs, or system failure. Planning for scalability from the outset ensures that the project can accommodate increasing demand while maintaining performance.

Scalability in Infrastructure: Projects like Uniswap encountered scalability challenges due to the rapid growth of their user base. Project managers must plan for the technical scalability of their blockchain infrastructure, whether that means adopting layer-2 scaling solutions, sharding, or increasing network capacity.

> *Practical Tip:* Incorporate scalability planning into the architecture phase. Explore solutions such as sidechains, layer-2 networks (e.g., Optimistic Rollups, zk-Rollups), or off-chain processing to enhance scalability without sacrificing decentralization.

Growth in User Base and Transactions: As the user base grows, so does the number of transactions, and the system must be able to handle increased traffic. If not managed properly, this can lead to slower processing times or even network congestion.

> *Practical Tip:* Design your system to accommodate both short-term and long-term growth. Implement stress testing early in the project to simulate high transaction volumes and identify potential bottlenecks before they occur.

By incorporating these best practices and strategies, project managers can replicate the success of previous blockchain implementations while adapting to the unique challenges of their own projects.

CHAPTER 7: The Future of Blockchain in Fintech

The fintech industry is experiencing a transformation that has the potential to reshape global finance. Blockchain, initially associated with cryptocurrencies like Bitcoin, has transcended its original use case and is now being viewed as a core technology that will drive the future of fintech. This chapter, as the final one in *Blockchain Blueprint: Project Management Strategies for Fintech Success*, will explore emerging trends such as Central Bank Digital Currencies (CBDCs). We will also consider how blockchain's innovations will fundamentally alter the whole of fintech project management.

The final chapter of this book serves as a combination of everything discussed, guiding readers through a future where blockchain isn't just a tool but an essential component of fintech success. As we discuss these trends, remember that understanding the full potential of blockchain is not merely a technological challenge but also a strategic imperative for project managers. In this period of rapid change, the key to staying ahead lies in being prepared to adapt and innovate.

Emerging Trends in Blockchain Technology

The blockchain ecosystem is evolving at a rapid pace. Several trends are emerging that hold significant promise for reshaping the financial sector and redefining how fintech companies operate. In addition to CBDCs and decentralized identities, we'll explore decentralized finance (DeFi), tokenization, and blockchain's intersection with artificial intelligence (AI).

1. Central Bank Digital Currencies (CBDCs)

CBDCs are not just another trend—they represent a fundamental shift in how governments and central banks think about money. A digital version of fiat currency issued by central banks, CBDCs bridge the gap between the world of blockchain and traditional financial systems. This technology enables faster, more secure, and transparent transactions, offering numerous benefits for both individuals and institutions.

Key Impacts of CBDCs:

Monetary Policy Innovation: CBDCs give central banks the ability to implement real-time monetary policy adjustments. Interest rates on CBDC accounts could be varied dynamically to influence spending and saving behaviors in an unprecedented way.

Cross-Border Payments: Cross-border transactions with traditional banks are often slow and expensive. CBDCs streamline this process, reducing transaction times from days to seconds. This is crucial for fintech companies that operate across borders and want to offer fast, low-cost payment solutions.

Programmable Money: CBDCs can enable the automation of certain financial activities. For instance, a government-issued CBDC could be programmed to only be used for specific purposes, like social welfare or disaster relief.

2. Decentralized Identity (DID)

The movement toward decentralized identity represents a radical departure from traditional, centralized systems of personal data management. DID enables individuals to have control over their personal information by using blockchain to store and verify identity in a decentralized manner. This not only enhances security but also eliminates intermediaries that are typically required to verify identity.

Decentralized Identity's Impact on Fintech:

Privacy-Enhancing Technologies (PETs): By allowing users to control their data, DID shifts the balance of power away from corporations and back to individuals. This could usher in a new era of privacy-first fintech applications, enabling services like loans, credit scoring, and payments without revealing sensitive personal information.

Interoperability Across Borders: DID standards are being designed to work across borders, facilitating global fintech applications. Whether it's a migrant worker sending money back home or a global traveler making purchases abroad, decentralized identities allow seamless verification.

Reduced Onboarding Time: For financial institutions, onboarding clients through traditional KYC processes is time-consuming and prone to errors. DID can automate and streamline these processes, significantly reducing onboarding times and enhancing customer experience.

3. Tokenization of Assets

Tokenization is the process of converting physical or digital assets into blockchain-based tokens. This can include everything from real estate to stocks, bonds, commodities, and even intellectual property. Tokenization is revolutionizing how value is created, stored, and transferred.

The Role of Tokenization in Fintech:

Fractional Ownership: By tokenizing assets, individuals can own fractional shares of high-value assets such as real estate or luxury goods. This opens up new investment opportunities for retail investors who were previously priced out of these markets.

Instant Settlement: Traditional asset transfers, such as buying real estate, can take weeks or even months to settle. Tokenized assets, when exchanged on a blockchain, allow for near-instant settlement. This reduces friction and costs in financial transactions.

Increased Liquidity: Tokenized assets can be traded on decentralized exchanges 24/7, providing liquidity in markets that are traditionally illiquid. For example, tokenized real estate shares could be sold instantly to other investors, improving market dynamics.

Challenges in Tokenization:

Regulatory Barriers: Tokenized assets straddle the line between traditional securities and digital assets. Fintech project managers must be keenly aware of securities regulations to avoid falling foul of the law.

Market Volatility: Tokenized assets, particularly those based on volatile markets like real estate or commodities, may experience sharp price fluctuations, complicating risk management.

4. Blockchain and Artificial Intelligence (AI) Integration

Blockchain and artificial intelligence (AI) are two of the most powerful technologies of the 21st century, and their intersection promises to bring new levels of efficiency and automation to fintech. AI can analyze large data sets, while blockchain ensures that this data is accurate, tamper-proof, and traceable.

Blockchain-AI Synergy in Fintech:

Automated Decision Making: AI can automate complex decision-making processes in real time, such as approving loans or managing risk. Blockchain ensures that the data feeding these AI models is trustworthy and immutable.

Enhanced Fraud Detection: AI-driven algorithms can identify patterns in financial data to detect fraudulent activity more accurately than humans. Blockchain can provide a secure audit trail, making it easier to track fraudulent activities across decentralized networks.

Predictive Analytics for Blockchain Networks: AI can predict potential bottlenecks or performance issues in blockchain networks by analyzing transaction data, thus improving network efficiency and scalability.

Project Management in Blockchain-AI Projects: Managing projects at the intersection of blockchain and AI requires deep expertise in both fields. Project managers will need to balance the complexities of AI model training with the robustness and security of blockchain systems. Moreover, ethical considerations, such as data privacy and algorithmic transparency, must be top of mind as fintech companies explore this space.

How Blockchain Will Shape the Future of Fintech Project Management

As we look ahead into the coming years, blockchain technology is set to reshape the very foundation of project management in the fintech industry. We are on the brink of a profound transformation—one where decentralization, automation, and immutability become integral elements of not just technological infrastructure but of the management philosophies that drive financial innovation. Project managers will need to adapt to a rapidly changing environment, equipped with new skills and tools designed to harness the power of blockchain.

Agile Methodologies

In the future, we anticipate that Agile will become the default methodology for managing blockchain projects. The volatile nature of both fintech markets and blockchain technology demands a level of flexibility that traditional project management frameworks simply cannot accommodate. Agile, with its iterative approach, will continue to gain prominence as it allows for rapid adaptation, helping teams to respond effectively to ever-changing regulations, technological breakthroughs, and shifting user expectations.

Blockchain projects will increasingly follow short sprints, each refining parts of decentralized systems or integrating new regulatory compliance measures. Developers, auditors, regulators, and financial analysts will collaborate in real-time, using Agile as a central framework to align cross-functional teams and streamline decision-making processes. We can expect to see decentralized Agile workflows powered by smart contracts, where team performance is automatically tracked and rewarded in real time through tokenized incentive structures.

This future marks a radical shift from today's slow-moving bureaucratic processes toward a more transparent, accountable, and rapidly evolving project management ecosystem. With blockchain as the backbone, project milestones will no longer rely on vague reports or arbitrary deadlines, but on verifiable achievements encoded directly onto the blockchain.

Smart Contracts and Automation

Looking further, the use of smart contracts to automate project management tasks will become the norm, not the exception. As more organizations integrate blockchain, the power of smart contracts to execute processes autonomously will take center stage. Imagine a future where project milestones are no longer tracked manually—where payments, resource allocation, and compliance audits all happen automatically.

Picture this: a global fintech firm runs a series of decentralized projects using a network of smart contracts. Each contract is tied to specific milestones, and as those milestones are met

—whether it's the successful implementation of a blockchain-based lending platform or the rollout of a new decentralized identity solution—funds are automatically disbursed, new project phases are unlocked, and deliverables are instantly recorded. No need for intermediaries, approvals, or administrative checks. Smart contracts will handle everything with the precision of code, enforcing rules without the risk of human error.

Project managers will be less focused on overseeing individual tasks and more on designing the logic that powers these contracts. Their role will shift from micromanagement to strategic oversight, crafting the blueprints that guide decentralized ecosystems toward successful outcomes. Blockchain will give rise to a new breed of project managers who are as proficient in writing smart contract code as they are in leading teams.

Risk Management and Governance

Taking it even deeper, and the role of risk management in fintech blockchain projects will take on an entirely new dimension. As blockchain's decentralized nature becomes more prevalent in financial systems, managing risks around security, scalability, and governance will no longer be a passive or reactive process. Instead, it will demand proactive, forward-looking strategies that leverage blockchain's transparency while also addressing its inherent vulnerabilities.

One of the biggest risks that fintech project managers will face in this new future is the threat of security breaches in decentralized ecosystems. The rise of quantum computing, for instance, could pose existential risks to current cryptographic protocols. In response, project managers will need to collaborate with cryptographers and cybersecurity experts to ensure that blockchain-based systems evolve to meet the challenges of this new computational power.

Similarly, governance in decentralized finance (DeFi) systems will grow more complex as these ecosystems scale. Project managers will need to navigate governance models that favor decentralization without sacrificing oversight. For example, decentralized autonomous organizations (DAOs) will require managers to devise governance frameworks that are both transparent and efficient. The future will see project managers moving away from top-down command structures and instead orchestrating complex, stakeholder-driven governance models that prioritize community input and trustless decision-making.

As governments increasingly issue regulations around blockchain, particularly in financial sectors, project managers will also need to become adept at balancing compliance with innovation. A future where regulators and blockchain developers work in tandem to create compliant, yet agile financial services is on the horizon, and project managers will be at the forefront of ensuring these partnerships thrive.

Scaling Blockchain

Scalability will remain one of the most pressing challenges in blockchain-based fintech. As we look into the future, we foresee breakthrough technologies that will address the scaling limitations of current blockchain systems. Layer 2 solutions, such as rollups and sidechains, will become the standard architecture for high-volume transaction processing in fintech applications.

Project managers of the future will no longer be bogged down by concerns over network congestion or high gas fees. Instead, they will oversee projects using scalable blockchains that can handle thousands, if not millions, of transactions per second. Emerging technologies like sharding and Proof of Stake (PoS) consensus mechanisms will vastly improve throughput while maintaining decentralization and security.

However, the responsibility of ensuring scalability will rest on the shoulders of project managers, who will need to plan ahead for system expansions and upgrades. Fintech firms will increasingly rely on project managers to evaluate the long-term viability of blockchain platforms, ensuring that as the user base grows, the technology remains both functional and cost-effective.

As we peer into the future of fintech project management, one thing is certain: blockchain is here to stay, and its influence will only deepen. Project managers will evolve from facilitators of linear tasks to orchestrators of decentralized, automated systems. They will be responsible for not only managing teams but also designing the very frameworks that empower blockchain-driven innovations. From smart contracts to decentralized governance, the future will demand a new skill set—one that embraces both technology and adaptability.

Those project managers who can anticipate and leverage blockchain's capabilities will thrive in a future defined by decentralization, automation, and transparency. The fintech landscape will be one of unparalleled innovation, and project managers who stay ahead of the curve will lead the charge in shaping the financial world of tomorrow. The revolution is just beginning, and blockchain is paving the way for a future where trust is built into every transaction, decision, and milestone.

Conclusion

As we conclude our exploration of blockchain's transformative potential within fintech, let's revisit the key takeaways that will equip you to navigate this dynamic landscape. Throughout this book, we've gone through the fundamental concepts of blockchain technology, its unique benefits, and the challenges it presents.

We hope that the strategies and insights shared in these pages have provided you with a solid foundation for managing blockchain projects successfully.

Thank you for joining us on this journey. By applying these principles, you can utilize blockchain to drive innovation, enhance efficiency, and shape the future of fintech.

Key Takeaways and Strategic Insights

Understanding Blockchain Fundamentals: Blockchain is a decentralized, distributed ledger technology that enhances transparency, security, and efficiency. By grasping its fundamental principles—such as consensus mechanisms, cryptographic hashing, and smart contracts—project managers can better appreciate how blockchain can transform various aspects of fintech.

Aligning Blockchain Solutions with Business Goals: The success of any blockchain initiative hinges on its alignment with the overarching business objectives of the organization. Project managers must assess the specific challenges within their organization and explore how blockchain can provide solutions. This alignment ensures that resources are invested wisely and that the project delivers measurable value.

The Importance of Collaboration and Communication: Effective communication among all stakeholders—developers, executives, regulators, and users—is vital for the success of blockchain projects. Building a culture of collaboration fosters trust and encourages the sharing of ideas, ultimately leading to more innovative and effective solutions.

Risk Management and Compliance: Navigating the regulatory landscape is a crucial aspect of managing blockchain projects in fintech. Project managers must be proactive in identifying potential risks, including legal and compliance issues. Establishing robust risk management frameworks and engaging with legal experts can help mitigate these risks and ensure adherence to regulations.

Adopting an Agile Approach: The rapid pace of technological change demands that project managers adopt agile methodologies. This flexibility allows teams to respond swiftly to emerging trends, user feedback, and market dynamics, ensuring that blockchain solutions remain relevant and effective.

Investing in Education and Skill Development: As the blockchain landscape evolves, continuous learning and skill enhancement become paramount. Organizations should prioritize training programs that equip team members with the knowledge and skills necessary to navigate this complex technology landscape.

Monitoring and Evaluation: Finally, establishing mechanisms for ongoing monitoring and evaluation is essential for assessing the performance of blockchain initiatives. By tracking key performance indicators (KPIs) and gathering user feedback, project managers can make informed decisions about future developments and enhancements.

Final Thoughts on Managing Blockchain Projects for Fintech Success

In this demanding world of fintech, where innovation and disruption are the norms, blockchain stands out as a transformative force. Its potential to streamline processes, enhance security, and reduce costs offers unprecedented opportunities for organizations willing to embrace it. However, with great potential comes significant responsibility.

As project managers, your role extends beyond mere execution; you are the architects of change within your organization. By applying the strategies and insights shared throughout this book, you can navigate the complexities of blockchain implementation, turning challenges into opportunities.

Embrace the mindset of continuous improvement. The journey doesn't end with the launch of a blockchain project; it's an ongoing process of adaptation, learning, and growth. As you engage with this technology, remain curious and open to new ideas. The fintech landscape is dynamic, and the organizations that thrive will be those that innovate, adapt, and inspire.

In conclusion, the successful management of blockchain projects in fintech requires a blend of technical knowledge, strategic foresight, and strong interpersonal skills. As you embark on this exciting journey, remember that the future of finance is being shaped by your efforts today. Be bold, be visionary, and embrace the future of blockchain in fintech.

ABOUT THE AUTHOR

Odunayo Akindote PMP, CSM, SSM

Odunayo Akindote is a Certified Blockchain Project Manager (CBPM), Certified Project Management Professional (PMP), and Certified Scrum Master (CSM) with a proven track record of delivering complex Technology Projects including blockchain and tokenomics across fintech and other industries. She plays a pivotal role in overseeing the planning, execution, and delivery of technology based project ensuring alignment with company goals and stakeholder requirements.

Her expertise blends *Agile project management skills *with a specialized understanding of blockchain technology, making her a key player in driving innovation and efficiency.